JONATHAN PINNOCK
England and read Math........... at Cambridge
University. He subsequently stumbled into a career in
software development and has been there ever since.
Somewhere along the way he wrote one book on
software development and co-wrote a further twelve
before he realised there were more interesting
subjects to write about. His short stories have been
widely published and his collection *Dot Dash* won the
Scott Prize, while his debut novel *Mrs Darcy versus the
Aliens* occasionally appears in lists of things that
should never have been done to Jane Austen. *Take It
Cool* is his first work of non-fiction that has nothing
to do with computers. He is married with two slightly
grown-up children and a 1961 Ami Continental Juke-
box. He blogs at www.jonathanpinnock.com and
tweets as @jonpinnock.

Previously by Jonathan Pinnock

Professional DCOM Application Development
Mrs Darcy versus the Aliens
Dot Dash

Take It Cool

*in search of the greatest
reggae singer you've never heard of*

by
Jonathan Pinnock

TWO RAVENS
P R E S S

Published by Two Ravens Press Limited
1, Fivepenny, Port of Ness, Isle of Lewis, HS2 0XG

The right of Jonathan Pinnock to be identified as author of
this work has been asserted by him in accordance with
the Copyright, Designs and Patent Act, 1988.

© Jonathan Pinnock, 2014

ISBN:978-1-906120-66-5

British Library Cataloguing in Publication Data: a CIP record
for this book can be obtained from the British Library.

Designed and typeset by Calum Kerr
Cover design by Hebridean Imaging
Printed in the EU

Contents

This book is dedicated to Pinnocks
everywhere, but especially
Gail, Mark and Rachel
and, of course, Dennis.

Two Consonants Away

Inheritance is a multi-faceted thing. If your parents are wealthy, there's a pretty good chance you won't go short of cash yourself. If they have healthy genes, you will almost certainly acquire a decent selection of those as well. But the only thing you are absolutely guaranteed to inherit is your parents' surname. And I'm going to stick my neck out and say that a good surname – at least in your formative years – is more important than either money or DNA. Because if you're born with a cool name, you'll be cool wherever you go. But if you're born with an uncool name, you'll *never* be cool.

I know all about this. I am a Pinnock.

If you're born with the surname Pinnock, you are just two consonants away from disaster, and that proximity pretty much wipes out any chance you have of being cool. There are no cool people in my family. There are quite a few strange people, sure, some eccentric ones and possibly even one or two mad ones, but no cool people whatsoever. Frankly, cool is pretty much out of the question, unless … unless … but I'm jumping ahead of myself.

This isn't to say I've never tried. At school, back at the start of the seventies, the cool people would walk around with an LP of impressively heavy music tucked conspicuously under their arm: 'In-a-Gadda-Da-Vida' by Iron Butterfly, 'Watt' by Ten Years After, 'Five Bridges' by The Nice, and so on. An LP was a substantial statement to be carrying around with you: a 12" square signal to the world saying what you felt about it, visible across the whole length of the playground.

Naturally, if you wanted to look cool like them and even be allowed to borrow one of their precious records, you had to buy one yourself. By now you may have guessed that I was the one who went out and bought the King Crimson album. No, not the cool first one with the far out cover; that one was already taken. I went out and bought the frankly rather lacklustre second one. I couldn't even manage imitation cool. And all I ever managed to borrow in return was Emerson, Lake and bloody Palmer and a couple of particularly pretentious Moody Blues albums.

So short of changing my name, I resigned myself to remaining uncool to the end of my days. Even if I did change my name, chances are that if you cut me open I'd have 'Pinnock' printed through my every bone like Brighton rock. There are some things you just can't run away from. But I still lived in hope.

And then one day everything changed.

In the early eighties I had a plan. I was young, free and single. I had a moderately well-paid job in software development. Life was an index of possibilities. So I decided that this was a really good time to get into the property market.

I didn't say it was a good plan.

Actually, it was worse than that. If I'd had half a brain cell active I would have bought myself a nice cosy flat in a pleasant neighbourhood. But I had bigger plans: I wanted to buy a *house*, a house that I could do up and make a tidy profit from. Yeah, this was definitely the eighties.

The problem was that I was working in London, so if I was going to buy a house it would have to be in one of the less fashionable areas of the city. Let's call this area Peckham for sake of argument. So with the help of a mortgage from the Abbey National Building Society, I did indeed buy myself a property in the unpromisingly-named Bellenden Road, Peckham.

As far as making a profit, it was a disaster. First of all, after seeing the inspection report, which ran to several volumes,

Abbey National decided – in a master stroke of counter-intuitivity – to withhold a significant amount of the mortgage until I'd fixed all the structural problems with the place. Secondly, the great wave of gentrification that was sweeping through south London took one look at Bellenden Road and the obscenity that was sheltering in its name and said: this far but no further.* The final insult came when I sold the place a few years later and a couple of prospective buyers noticed something unusual stuck in the back fence – or, rather, the few nailed-together sheets of hardboard that passed for a fence that I hadn't got around to replacing. 'Ooh, look,' they said, having identified the object, 'Integral dead cat.'

But I liked Bellenden Road. I liked Peckham. It was diverse. It was full of real life. On the night I moved in, I nipped across the road to the pub and was impressed to observe two separate fights break out. A different pub on a different night was clearly the location for a high-level gangland rendezvous, at least if the selection of top-of-the-range motors parked around the block was anything to go by. By complete contrast, the pub around the other corner was largely frequented by resting film extras.

It also had some excellent junk shops.

One fine Saturday morning, not long after I'd moved in, I was idly mooching around one of these and noticed that they had a selection of scratchy singles for sale at bargain prices. Well, I'm a sucker for a bit of cheap tat, and I had a brief rummage. And on that day, I experienced something of an epiphany.

The record was called 'Take It Cool', on Venture Records. And the artist's name was – joy of joys – Dennis Pinnock. I turned it over. Even better, the flipside was called 'Pinnock's

---

* Or at least it did while I was living there. At the time of writing, however, my house's estimated value has apparently ballooned to twenty-five times what I paid for it, so things have clearly changed. This isn't by any means an isolated example of bad financial timing on my part.

Paranormal Payback'. How cool was that? It was worth at least a hundred times the 10p that I paid for it.

Much to my surprise, the music didn't disappoint. 'Take It Cool' was a very satisfying slice of that smooth sub-genre of reggae known as Lovers Rock – it was a decent production and the singer clearly knew how to carry a tune. However, 'Pinnock's Paranormal Payback' was wonderful. It was – inevitably – a dub version of 'Take It Cool'. How much better could this get? I *love* dub. The central principle seems to be to take the master tapes of the main feature, skin up a two-foot long spliff of Jamaica's finest and then press whatever buttons come into your head. When it works, it's fabulous. When it doesn't, at least you know that someone was having a good time when they made it. And 'Pinnock's Paranormal Payback' was *fabulous*.

So, Dennis Pinnock, eh? Here, at last, was a cool Pinnock. Unexpectedly, he was clearly also a black Pinnock. So the moral appeared to be that to be cool *and* a Pinnock, you also had to be black. Unfortunately, what limited research I'd done on the subject had led me to the deeply disappointing conclusion that I have no non-Caucasian blood in me whatsoever. In fact, the nearest I had ever come to West Indian culture was an evening spent drinking Red Stripe in Bradford's notorious Coconut Club, a place so gloriously stereotypical that the dealers wore three-piece suits and the undercover cops wore Afghans. But that's another story altogether.

The Pinnock side of my family emerged from the West Country a couple of generations back, and – given the historic levels of in-breeding prevalent in that part of the world – it wasn't unreasonable to assume that it was West Country all the way back to the dawn of man. This all left a couple of nagging questions. First of all, who the hell was this Dennis Pinnock? Did he make any more records? Was he a big star somewhere?

Secondly, what the hell was he doing with my surname?

Googling Dennis

Actually, it didn't really happen like that at all. 'Take It Cool' sat in the middle of my collection of 45's – somewhere between 'Papa's Gotta Brand New Pigbag' by, well, Pigbag and 'Gimme Dat Ding' by The Pipkins – for the next twenty or so years, whilst I moved out of Peckham, got married and had a couple of kids. Every now and then, I would take it out and play it for amusement, assuming that I'd never in a million years find out any more about the singer.

And then one day, round about the time when the new millennium reached school age, it suddenly struck me that Dennis Pinnock was now Googleable. So I hit the web and found to my surprise that he'd actually been quite prolific – although a picture slowly began to emerge of someone who'd clearly been forever on the cusp of breaking through but had never quite managed it. Interestingly, whenever his records turned up on eBay – and I had set up a watch on him right from the start – I got the impression that they were quite sought after. Then again, I may have just been taken in by the sales pitch, because now I come to think about it, I never did seem to run into a lot of competition whenever I bid for one.

By the time I'd finished (and it took me several years of fastidious eBay monitoring), I'd amassed no less then sixteen twelve-inch singles (OK, eighteen, except one was a grey-vinyl special edition and another turned out on closer inspection to be a swap), plus a further three seven-inchers, including the original 'Take It Cool' that had started this all off. I also picked up a couple of twelve-inch singles by a band called *Four in a Row*, one of whom was none other than our man Pinnock, another by a group with the excellent name of Eargasm which also turned out to have him as a member, and a duet by 'Dennis and Lauraine'. Finally, I picked up a sampler CD featuring four of the tracks from his singles along with work by other artists. Very few of the singles had dates on them, and there was no information on the CD at all beyond track titles and the names of artist and producer.

Now in any other area of popular music, you'd think that someone who had managed to put his name on over twenty singles (to say nothing of a grey vinyl special edition), in the course of a career spanning three decades, would have graduated to an album career at some point. Indeed, there is a tantalising glimpse of what might have been on the centre label of 'The Feeling', where it proclaims: 'Taken from Forthcoming LP "Dennis the Menace"'. But no such album ever turned up in my searches. It seems that something must have gone wrong at the last minute.

Indeed, if you look closer, the picture becomes murkier still. Those twenty-odd singles are on no less than a dozen different labels. Sometimes he only appears on one side of a single, with someone completely different on the other. Misspellings abound – including his own name, which is given as 'Dennis Pinock' on the hastily-drawn picture sleeve of 'Ride On'. Either he was a particularly difficult man to deal with or he had been very badly served indeed by the recording industry.

Whatever the true story was, I needed to know more about this guy.

Prevarication and Procrastination

By now, I'm guessing you may be asking one of two key questions, depending on where you're coming from. Either you're wondering why on earth a middle-aged, middle-class white guy like myself would be so intrigued by the idea of a black reggae singer with the same stupid surname, or you're thinking, 'Wow! That's amazing!' and wondering why it took me so long to get my act together and find out more. The truth is that the two questions are inextricably linked, bound together by a third one which essentially boils down to this: what the hell did I think I was playing at?

Maybe I was simply doing the same kind of thing that anyone who conducts any research into their family tree is doing: desperately trying to find something – anything! – interesting in their genes. To be honest, I've tended to sneer at this kind of thing in the past, being of the opinion that it's up to you to make something of yourself and not rely on your ancestors to do the work for you. If that makes me sound like a pompous git, well maybe we should make that a pompous, hypocritical git, because with this project I was actually committing a far worse offence than that. I was trying to *invent* some kind of exotic connection in my past, for God's sake.

In any case, what was I going to do if I managed to track Dennis Pinnock down? Did I really want to meet him? What would I say to him? What would he say to me? Did I even have the faintest idea how to go about such a search at all? And would it take me into scary places? With scary people?

All of that was going through my mind when I was debating

whether or not to go any further with this. I wondered for a while if there was some kind of racial element to it. Was my motive for embarking on the project a desire to exorcise some latent racism lurking in my psyche? Or – awful thought – was that latent racism holding me back from going through with it? I'd certainly describe myself as a liberal kind of chap, but I would also have to admit that my circle of friends has a pretty high proportion of white people in it. In my youth, I certainly served time in many places that were institutionally racist; indeed, *Little Black Sambo* was one of the set texts at my primary school.*

In the end, though, I think the reason why I struggled for years to take this project by the horns was less to do with any racial thing than my general awkwardness when dealing with people, especially strangers. Let me try to elucidate: I'm six foot five in my M&S days-of-the-week socks, but my co-ordination stopped keeping pace when I was about four foot two. I move around the place like a man who's borrowed a rental body for the weekend and wasn't listening when they explained how all the parts worked. The top of my skull has evolved to be roughly twice the national average thickness, so many times have I bashed it on doors and ceilings. Grace and poise are alien concepts to me. (Oh, and in case you're wondering, days-of-the-week socks are a *very* bad idea. Every day is an obsessive-compulsive nightmare as you search for a pair that match not only each other but also the calendar. Don't buy them. Ever.)

It's not just physical awkwardness: I struggle to find the

---

* Funny thing about *Little Black Sambo*, by the way. I recently came across a couple of Helen Bannerman's other books, *Little Black Mingo* and *Little Black Quasha* in a second hand shop, and it wasn't until I looked at the weird illustrations of composite non-white people that it dawned on me that they were actually set in India, not – as I'd previously assumed – Africa. There were, after all, tigers in the pictures. Quite apart from the casual racism, I have a strong suspicion that these books may have wrecked an entire generation's understanding of zoology.

necessary mental co-ordination required to sustain a sensible conversation with a newcomer, whilst simultaneously trying to pick up on all the other non-verbal cues that are flying around. It's true that having a glass of wine in one hand can help with this, but this only works if I manage to keep it upright and avoid emptying its contents over the other party. In short, I've never been a man who's at ease with himself, which means that any endeavour even tangentially approaching investigative journalism is fraught with angst.

But something told me this was too good a story to run away from. I had no idea where it might lead, but I'd kick myself if I didn't at least follow it some of the way. The easiest part was the music itself, so that's where I started.

Dennis and the Last King of Scotland

Like many bookish, introverted kids of my generation, I used to collect stamps. Actually, that bald statement doesn't really do justice to it. I was more than a collector. I was a *curator*. I graded my collection into Premier Countries, Major Countries, Minor Countries and Mini Countries, according to the number of stamps that I had for each one. Australia, for some reason, had a whole album to itself. With cover-leaves. Great Britain and one or two others went into Premier Countries, in a nice smart loose-leaf album. Major Countries (such as Argentina and South Africa) and Minor Countries (such as France and Italy) were in decent loose-leaf albums. Mini Countries (the dross) were thrown into a home-made album made out of left-over loose leaves and a cardboard cover.

For Premier Countries, I would spend hours planning the layout. Think about it for a moment. That didn't just mean looking up each set in Stanley Gibbons and working out the most symmetrical arrangement (and bear in mind that more often than not, I wouldn't have a complete set to start with anyway), but it meant leaving suitably-sized gaps for the sets that I didn't have any of at all. I'm not knocking stamp collecting, by the way; it's a great way of learning all sorts of useless facts about the world, although for years I went under the impression that the fact that South African stamps were bilingual ('South Africa'/ 'Suid Afrika') was something to do with this awful apartheid thing that grown-ups seemed to go on about a lot.

Looking back, I can do the psychology – I was a timid child, struggling to deal with the big wide world, and collecting and organising a stamp collection was probably my way of imposing my own order on things. Trouble is, once a collector, always a collector, and this extends to music more than anything else. If I like someone's music, I tend to want to have everything by them, however awful – which is how I end up with things like 'Mingus' by Joni Mitchell in my CD collection. And don't get me started on King Crimson; when they launched the bloody 'King Crimson Collector's Club', those bastards saw me coming.* So you can imagine how pleased I was when, after years of searching, I finally acquired every single release that Dennis Pinnock had ever recorded. However, I was now faced with the second problem that faces every collector: putting it into some kind of order. This turned out to be another matter entirely. Only a few of them had a date on them, for one thing, and it was clear from those dates that were present that his recording career spanned more than a decade (at least 1977 to 1988), so I couldn't even hazard a guess. The other complication was to determine when his stints in Eargasm and Four in a Row fitted in, along with the Dennis and Lauraine duet.

For quite some time, I was convinced that Dennis Pinnock's very first appearance on vinyl was in 1977, on Conflict Records (7" black vinyl, catalogue number CON 305). The label design is quite striking: a pair of crossed swords,** with – at the point of contact – one of those jagged-edged balloons that usually contain the word 'ZAP!' or 'POW!', but in this case simply 'CONFLICT'. This, then, is an angry label from an angry time: 1977, the Year of

---

* As did whoever decided that the spines of the deluxe eight-double-CD Marillion reissue series should spell M-A-R-I-LL-I-O-N if you put them side by side. I only wanted the first one – mainly for the epic Grendel on the bonus CD – and inevitably I ended up buying the lot. I do not need eight Marillion double CDs. No-one does. Not even Marillion's respective mothers.

**Fans of architecture will be reminded of the *Swords of Qādisīyah* victory arch in Baghdad, which were – according to the authoritative reference book *Crap Towns* – cast in a foundry in Basingstoke.

Punk. The writing credits are divided between Ellis and Pinnock, with production by 'A. Ellis', and the more reggae-savvy readers among you will immediately be wondering whether this might in fact be Alton Ellis (1938 – 2008), also known as the 'Godfather of Rocksteady'. However, I'm going to keep you in suspense about that one for a little while.

The content of the record is eccentric, to say the least. I would go as far as to say that of the many singles in my collection, it is definitely one of the oddest. For a start, the title of the A side is 'IDI-AMIN' and the B side is called 'IDI-DUB'. Now I'm used to seeing references to Haile Selassie a.k.a. the Lion of Judah pop up all over the place when you start listening to reggae, but I hadn't expected to encounter the Last King of Scotland.* However, that's just the start of the weirdness. Before the music kicks in, Pinnock starts with a bold proclamation:

Anti propaganda!
Spread no propaganda 'bout Uganda!

The voice is a little rough, and (to be frank) a massive disappointment compared with the sweet delivery that I was familiar with from 'Take It Cool'. He isn't actually called upon to do much in the way of singing and what he does is probably closer to DJ-style toasting, but he manages to do it efficiently enough. However, the first thing that strikes you about 'IDI-AMIN' as you listen to it is the accompaniment seems awfully familiar. And then it hits you. Oh. My. God. That's the chord sequence from 'Lovin' You'. Minnie Riperton's 'Lovin' You'.

Not only that, but A. Ellis has overlaid this accompaniment

---

* Remarkably, this isn't the only song in Conflict's small but perfectly-formed discography to reference Amin. The very next record in their 11-disc catalogue, according to Discogs, is COND 2000, a 12" entitled 'Idi Amin Disco'/'Blood Up' by Militant (Barry). Even more remarkably, it has nothing whatsoever in common, either musically or lyrically, with Dennis Pinnock's record.

with a truly horrible birdsong effect. As you will no doubt remember, the second-most striking thing about the original 'Lovin' You' (after the late Ms Riperton's extraordinary five-and-a-half-octave voice) is the birdsong twittering along in the background. Dedicated fans of The Barron Knights may also be familiar with their parody, in which the bird is gradually joined by an increasingly bizarre selection of farmyard animals, but at least they didn't resort to effects such as the one deployed here. It is quite remarkably annoying.

Be that as it may, Pinnock continues with his song, the content of which appears to relate to the Queen's refusal to allow Idi Amin (then President of Uganda) to attend the celebrations for her Silver Jubilee:

Amin want to come fe the Jubilee
Amin want to come fe the Jubilee
Babylon a-try keep 'im out
Me say, Babylon a-try keep 'im out
De Babylon Queen done a-scream and shout

And so on. I do like that line about the Babylon Queen, but I have to say that it's a pretty bizarre choice of cause to get behind. In fact if you were to draw up a list of causes that really were not worth bothering to devote any time to whatsoever, I think this one would have to be pretty close to the top, especially when you consider that at the very same time, Johnny Rotten and his mates were taking criticism of the monarchy to a slightly more vitriolic and somewhat less specific level.

As I said, it's a truly bizarre record. After all that, the B side is a bit disappointing. It promises to be a dub, but actually it's exactly the same as the A side with the vocals removed. This basically has the effect of making that birdsong noise sound even more irritating than you thought possible.

Sadly, it seems that contemporary opinion was not wholly favourable either. While the review of 'Idi Amin' in *Black Music* magazine is in the 'BM's 10 Gold Tips' section, it damns it with faint praise by remarking that it is 'undoubtedly destined for the same cult status as "Eunoch Powell"* – despite the idiotic and misinformed theme.' It goes on to describe the lyrics as 'hoodwinked' and 'stupid' but charitably adds that it's 'toasted superbly – and a great dancer.' A later article on Conflict records notes that 'during its brief lifespan the label has already produced four highly successful albums' plus several top selling singles, before mentioning – somewhat unnecessarily in my opinion – that 'only one of their releases, Dennis Pinnock's "Idi Amin", has died the death.'

It has to be said that there have been more auspicious debuts in the history of music

---

* This would seem to be a reference to Errol Dunkley's 1976 single, 'Eunoch Power'.

How I Became an Internet Stalker

The real story, however, was Dennis Pinnock himself. I had to get my act together and start searching, because neither of us were getting any younger and anecdotal actuarial evidence suggested that the life expectancy of people in the music business in general (and the reggae business in particular) wasn't exactly in the higher percentiles.

The most recent sighting of him was on a handbill that I'd nabbed from somewhere on the internet back when I'd started tinkering around with my quest. Brilliantly, I'd managed to save the JPEG with no details whatsoever of where I'd got it from, and subsequent searches have failed to find it again. Never mind. The event that the handbill was advertising took place on January 11th, 2002, at the East Oxford Community Centre in Oxford, presented by 'Roots n Culture, The Friendly Reggae Community'. The event itself is described as 'An Ethiopian Christmas & Capricorn's Reggae Birthday Party', along with the advice to 'remember to invite all your Capricorn friends, this is their birthday party'.

Dennis is some way down the bill, as the headline spot is shared between King Original ('East London's Legendary Roots Sound System – Established 1973') and Roots Commandment ('Roots Sound System From Hamburg, Germany'). The rest of the line-up is listed under the somewhat dismissive heading of 'Also Live Roots Singers', and consists of Errol Bellot, Chanter, Dixie Peach, African Simba, Colourman, Dennis Pinnock, G Vibes + More.

The next logical step was to hunt for more information on his fellow performers, and it turned out that several of them had a decent-enough profile, at least within the world of reggae, although none of them had managed to break into the mainstream. Errol Bellot, for example, had a string of hits in the 80s, starting with the roots anthem 'Babylon'. Afrikan (sic) Simba seems to have been quite prolific as well, according to an extensive profile in *Reggae News*, with one album out and several more in the pipeline. Dixie Peach – not to be confused with the Norwegian Southern Rock (yes, really) band with the same name – has also had several worldwide reggae hits to his name, including a number one with the splendidly-titled 'Ragga Muffin and Rambo'.

Chanter and Colourman, however, proved impossible to track down. Rule number one, guys: if you want to make a name for yourself, try to make it one that's Googleable. But G Vibes turned out to be easier to find, with his own Myspace page, along with some surprising alternative sites to investigate that Google threw up. I guess that G Vibes wasn't to know this when he adopted his stage name, but generally speaking I would counsel against sharing your moniker with that of a vibrating cock ring. Still, what do I know? I am, after all, still a Pinnock.

As I looked at the lists of names of the people these guys had worked with, I kept coming across people I'd bumped into before in connection with Dennis: guys like Sugar Minott, Tex Johnson and Alton Ellis. What I really needed right now, more than anything, was one of those Pete Frame rock family trees, but I guess he's probably wise enough never to have attempted such a thing for the world of reggae. If he had, he'd probably still be working on it to this day – all over the walls of a padded cell.

Still, I had a few names to start with and I was now in a position to draw up a spreadsheet of people to attempt to contact. I like spreadsheets. There's nothing quite like a bit of Excel to add a convincing veneer of organisation to an otherwise chaotic and hopeless endeavour. However, simply putting a few names in boxes wasn't helping me to get in touch with any of them. Then it struck me that one of my potential targets was on Myspace. You could message people on Myspace. Admittedly, I'd have to get a Myspace account to do that, but that was a price I'd have to pay. (Jesus H. Christ. Myspace? Hahahahahaha.)

But then I had another thought. Facebook. I *bet* they're on Facebook! *Everyone's* on Facebook, aren't they? Obviously I started by searching for Dennis himself, but nothing useful came up; I was going to have to work a bit harder. However, Errol Bellot turned out to have a personal account as well as a fan page, which was promising. And checking through his list of friends, I spotted Afrikan Simba Tukur Anbessa straight away, along with Chanter Anderson (who I took to be the mysterious 'Chanter' from the Oxford gig) as well as Dixie Peach. I also happened to notice Burning Spear. Burning Spear! That would be Burning Spear, who recorded the bona fide classic 'Marcus Garvey' album, would it not? It most certainly was. Wow. This guy certainly had some seriously cool friends. No sign of Dennis himself, though – that would have been too easy.

So the next step was to message each of the performers that I'd found. Sadly, Dixie Peach's account was locked down to the extent that he was neither accepting friend requests nor receiving messages – so essentially he'd taken out Facebook's equivalent of a pre-emptive restraining order against nutters like me. But the other three were all open to being messaged. So that's exactly what I did. This is what I sent out:

Hi,

I wonder if you can help me. I'm a writer doing some research on a book and I'm trying to find out about Dennis Pinnock, the singer. The reason I'm approaching you, incidentally, is because I believe you were on the same bill as him at an event in Oxford in January 2002. Is he still alive? Are you in touch with him? Is he contactable? I'd be most grateful for any information you can provide.

Which was probably a bit stuffy, now I come to look at it again. To make matters worse, my Facebook cover photo at the time showed me gurning at the camera, leaning on a signpost pointing to the hamlet of St Pinnock in Cornwall (of which more later). In addition to this, my timeline header consisted of a banner advertising my first book *Mrs Darcy versus the Aliens,* so it's possible that I may not have been giving the right impression. It also struck me that if you read the message in a hurry you might mistakenly infer that it was seeking information on a cold case, with the unstated implication that a badly decomposed body had recently been dug up somewhere in Cowley.

But it was at least worth a shot. I also swallowed my pride and joined Myspace as well, sending the same message to G Vibes, although I have to say I wasn't hopeful about this one at all, because he hadn't updated his page since 2010. And it was sodding Myspace, for heaven's sake. Either way, the messages had gone out and all I could do now was sit and wait for someone to reply.

The Wrong Corner of the Triangle

The next conundrum was to work out how the Pinnock surname had ended up attached to Dennis, and for want of any idea of where to start, I decided I might as well have a dig around in my family's past. I didn't know an awful lot about the early history on the Pinnock side, apart from the fact that both my paternal grandparents started off life as teachers in Bristol, and that my great-grandfather was called Joseph Brown Pinnock. I only knew this because he died a week or so before my father was born, and thus managed to bequeath to him his entire name, including that rather curious 'Brown' bit. However, Brown or no Brown, there didn't seem to be any clues there as to how the name could have crossed the race boundary.

My initial, somewhat naïve, thought was to find some ancestor or other who might have travelled a bit, perhaps stopping off in the West Indies for a bit of r'n'r and wild oat-sowing on the way. The first candidate was my Great Uncle Arthur, who had apparently worked for an overseas trading company, and had indeed travelled the world in a big way. He never married, earned a considerable amount of money but was rumoured to have left hardly a penny when he died. Unfortunately he lived from 1882 to 1950, which meant that – given the apparently enormous number of West Indian Pinnocks that were beginning to turn up in my searches – he would have had to have been an extraordinarily busy man during his fertile years. So reluctantly I ruled him out.

The next possibility was Joseph Brown Pinnock (I) himself, given that he was the current limit of my knowledge. Intriguingly, he did cross the Atlantic, in 1871, to try to start a new life in Canada – a project which presumably didn't come to anything, because he came back five years later. But once again, given that he was born in 1851 and died in 1916, he was too recent to be implicated. He was also a particularly unlikely candidate in the wild oats area, because he was sufficiently well-regarded in his local Methodist community to have been presented with a bible on the occasion of his departure for the Americas, although I guess that's not necessarily a 100% cast-iron guarantee of probity.

If I wanted to go any further back, I would have to carry out some proper genealogical research, in which case my first port of call would probably be the family grave. Yes, it turned out that in Portishead cemetery, just down the road from Bristol, there is indeed a Pinnock family grave, apparently unused since the days of Joseph Brown himself. Oddly, when I searched for Portishead Cemetery on Google, I got a sponsored link asking me if I wanted to buy a Bristol cemetery on eBay. Sadly, zero items were found, but I saved the link to my favourites just in case.

However, by this time, a more sinister possibility was beginning to form in my mind. Bristol was once one of the two key British ports in the triangular Atlantic slave trade. From here, the ships left for the coast of Western Africa, loaded with muskets and other manufactured goods. Having exchanged these for slaves, they would set sail for the rich plantations of the West Indies. The final exchange would be for commodities such as sugar and cotton, which would be sold back in the home country. A gruesomely efficient economic system, offering a profit at each stage of the journey. And unpleasant though the thought was, it was not beyond the bounds of possibility that one of my Bristolian ancestors could have been involved. It was certainly something that I needed to look into, and almost straight away I hit paydirt.

What I found was some correspondence from James and

Philip Pinnock, shipping agents in Jamaica, to one Samuel Munckley. This consisted of a covering letter for an invoice and a bill of lading for sugar – in other words, the cargo carried on the final, homeward-bound leg of the triangle. The letter was dated July 2nd, 1773. I was quite excited at this – that is, until I realised that it was telling me something much more complicated. What it was saying was that in the late eighteenth century, the white Pinnocks were already established in Jamaica. I was looking at the wrong corner of the triangle.

This opened up a whole new strand of investigation. I needed to find out more about Philip and James Pinnock – who were they and were they the ones who were responsible for introducing the name to the West Indies? I also wanted to see if I could somehow tie them back to Bristol, and hence to my ancestors. Given the nature of what was emerging, I was beginning to get a little anxious about what I might find, but it had to be done.

Idi Amin is Really Loving You

Back at the discography, I was now faced with having to deal with the thorny issue of whether 'IDI-AMIN' actually was Dennis Pinnock's debut record. What made me change my mind about this was the discovery of a version of 'Loving You' (sic) by Janet Kay, with the B side by none other than Dennis. Janet Kay is a recording artist of some distinction, known these days as 'The Queen of Lovers Rock', although her main claim to fame is her breakthrough hit 'Silly Games', which reached No 2 in the UK singles charts in 1979. 'Silly Games' is a gorgeous record, notable for that heart-stopping moment when the line about 'having no time to play your silly games' makes a sharp left turn into the minor key and she launches into an unexpected falsetto.

'Loving You' is on the 'All Tone' label (12", catalogue number AT006), which appears to be Alton Ellis' own label, for his name appears on the credits as producer and arranger. So that at least answers our question about the identity of A. Ellis. Sadly, Ms Kay's first name is given as 'Janett', but according to the discography on her own website it was her first-ever recording, so she probably wasn't too bothered. There is no credit given to either Minnie Riperton or her co-writer Richard Rudolph, and in fact the title is misspelled too (it's actually 'Lovin' You'), but never mind. The key question is: what does it sound like?

What it sounds like, unexpectedly, is Dennis Pinnock's 'IDI-AMIN'. The backing track is, in fact, EXACTLY the same one that's used on the other record, including that godawful tweeting. The vocal is a little disappointing, too. Given the range displayed on 'Silly Games', you might think Janet Kay would have been the ideal choice to do a reggae cover of 'Lovin' You', but the curious thing is that, two years before her big hit, she doesn't really go for it. Maybe the relative failure of that one convinced her to try a bit harder – who knows?

Turning the record over, we find the enigmatically-named 'Version' by Dennis Pinnock. And as we play it, we realise with a sinking heart that this is in fact 'IDI-AMIN' again, with the disappointing difference that it goes on a bit longer. So how on earth did this come to happen? Let's imagine the conversation.

'Hey, Dennis? It's Alton. You know you wanted to be a big star?'

'Er, yeah?'

'Well, I'm doing a session with Janet – you remember her, yeah? – and we're short of a B side.'

'Can't you just do a dub?'

'Nah. Doesn't really work. We're doing a version of that "Loving You" thing. Got anything that might fit?'

'Well, I've got this sort of toast-y thing about Idi Amin not being allowed to come to the jubilee – '

'Um … right. Yeah, right. Whatever. Two o'clock OK for you?'

I couldn't really think of any other way it could have happened. Neither could I work out how the same song ended up on the A side of a completely different label. The fact remains, however, that Dennis Pinnock started off his career working alongside two of the biggest names in black British music. The odd thing is that his music actually got a lot better, but while Janet Kay went on to much higher things, he somehow got left behind.

This wasn't the last I was to hear of 'IDI-AMIN' a.k.a. 'Loving You', incidentally. I'd decided that I probably needed to get a more thorough overview of Lovers Rock, and that the best place to start would be to get hold of the appropriate Trojan Records box set. I'm a big fan of those 50-track, 3-CD Trojan compilations, even if they are essentially the lazy person's way to collect reggae, relying on Trojan's massive clout to license as near as dammit definitive cross sections of a given subset of the genre. The Christmas one in particular is a brilliant alternative to Phil Spector if you're finding him a bit creepy these days, even if the lyrical content of a considerable number of the tracks essentially boils down to 'All I Want For Christmas Is A Big Fat Spliff'. Unfortunately, they tend to be limited editions and the Lovers Rock one had sold out, so I was reduced to paying way over the odds for a slightly foxed secondhand one, trying not to be too put off by the presence of a faux lipstick kiss on the pink and mauve box design.

Sadly there were no selections from Dennis Pinnock's oeuvre in there, but I was rather stunned to notice that the very first track on CD 1 was 'Lovin' You' by Janet Kay (noting in passing that both the singer and the song were spelt correctly this time, and that the songwriters were both now properly credited). It's a slightly shorter version than the one on the 12" single that we heard back in Chapter Three and I'm convinced the birdsong is less prominent in the mix, but it's definitely the same production. My God. Dennis Pinnock could have been on there instead if he hadn't misread the signs and gone for an overtly political lyric. Because that was, after all, the whole raison d'être of Lovers Rock: it was a reaction to the increasing politicisation of mainstream reggae. Lovers Rock was a return to the basics of pop, back to a simpler world of boy meets girl. Dennis Pinnock seems to have cottoned on to this pretty quickly, as his later records show, but the sad fact is that his very first recording – on a record produced by the great Alton Ellis, remember – might have been his best opportunity to make his mark.

Pain and Disappointment

When you're researching your family tree, it's hard not to get depressed as you realise that the vast majority of lives seem to end in either pain or disappointment or indeed – all too often – both. Here's the start of what looks like a typewritten circular letter from the owner of my great-grandfather's last place of employment, S. M. Wilmot, on the occasion of his death:

> DEAR SIR,
>
> *It is with very deep regret that I have to inform you of the death of my friend, Mr. J. B. PINNOCK. He passed away on the 10th inst (after being a great sufferer), at his residence, Beech Road, Portishead...*

As I read it, that phrase – almost an afterthought – 'after being a great sufferer' leapt out at me. At least it wasn't that old canard about a long illness bravely borne; I know that if a long terminal illness awaits me, it will be borne with extreme cowardice on my part and massive irritation on the part of everyone around me.

I wondered if he'd had the luxury of knowing he was on his way out, or if they had decided to withhold the nature of his condition from him. He was a man, so I guess they would have been pretty straight with him. My mother wasn't so fortunate. For reasons best known to the professionals entrusted with her care, it was deemed that my father should keep her illness secret until a couple of weeks or so before she died. Looking back on it, she must have known what was up, even when fed a continual intravenous drip of false hope; no-one is that dumb, especially my mother of all people. And as you may imagine, she was extremely angry when my father finally broke the news, although she did face up to her end with remarkable dignity – yes, bravery in fact. She even tried to tell me herself that she was dying, but I wasn't ready to hear it yet and she was too ill to try again after that.

My father, on the other hand, was never really quite the same again after almost a year of deception, even though he remarried and lived on for another three and a half decades. In keeping with the general policy of running away from death, I was packed off for the weekend when she actually died. I'd not long turned sixteen and I was thought to be too young to have to cope with it all, although God knows I'd watched her being reduced from a tall, vibrant woman to a parchment and bone husk over the previous few weeks. It's getting on for forty years since it happened, and it's still raw. What I hate most of all, to the core of my being, is that my strongest memories of her are on her death bed: those pathetic, hateful images that get in the way of everything else. Is that unusual, or is it the same for all of us?

I wonder what she would have made of this project: complete bemusement, I suspect. Bless her, wherever she is.

I was now fully engaged with the task of working backwards from Joseph Brown Pinnock (I), in the hope of joining up the family trees at some point with the Jamaican branch I'd just come across. My father and uncle had both dabbled a bit in genealogical research, but stupidly I'd failed to get any information of real value from either of them whilst they were still alive. All I had was a box full of papers, plus some additional notes made by my father and some scribbles in my own handwriting that I could barely read, dating from the one occasion I tapped him for some family anecdotes. The latter was essentially a whole load of semi-coherent non-sequiturs, such as 'Auntie Lil – social climber, name-dropper – married Uncle Arnold – cement, managed <illegible> in Jabalpur (?) (India), also S. America, "couldn't afford to retire as Auntie Lil spent so much", "you don't call it Golf, you call it Gawlf" and so on. This was another of those many occasions when it's struck me that we didn't talk nearly enough, my father and I: two awkward, clumsy blokes with very little in common that either of us would admit to.

My first port of call would therefore have to be that Portishead family grave. I must admit that the idea of a family grave strikes me as a bit odd, mainly because I find the idea of graves a bit odd *per se*. That's not to say that I haven't presided over several informal, non-denominational interment ceremonies for much-loved family pets in my time – and, indeed, subsequent re-interment on more than one occasion following desecration by vandals from the local fox community. But as far as I'm concerned, I'm not too bothered what happens to my corporeal remains. Recycle what you can, give any unusual bits to research and feed the rest to the dog. If you insist on cremation, at least try and scatter my ashes somewhere unusual or inconvenient, but preferably not in a graveyard. However, if you really must, make it a cool place of burial, preferably with a soundtrack of Beth Gibbons warbling over a trip-hop backdrop. A Portishead cemetery, in fact.

So I e-mailed the folks in charge of the cemetery, and they got back to me with the following information:

Upon checking our records I can confirm that there is a Pinnock family grave in Portishead Cemetery.

The grave reference is Section L Number 68, deceaseds' details as follows-

Joseph Brown Pinnock - Aged 64 - Died 9/8/1916 - Buried 12/8/1916
Mary Jane Pinnock - Aged 73 - Died 9/2/1930 - Buried 12/2/1930
Henry John Pinnock - Ashes casket buried - 21/10/1951
Mary Kathleen Doris Pinnock - Aged 95 - Died 20/11/1992 - Ashes buried - 8/12/1992

To be honest, I'd been hoping for something a bit more well-stocked, but it still seemed worth a visit.

Dennis Makes a Massive Attack

Moving on in our trek through the tortuous landscape of Dennis Pinnock's recording career, we're about to arrive at a plateau of relative stability. In 1978 he seems to have formed a working relationship with a producer called D. Tyrone, who also turns out to have been the owner of the Gangsterville Musical Arcade, situated at 994 Harrow Road, NW10, from 1974 to 1981. You might be forgiven for thinking that NW10 seems a long way from the Brixton heartland of London West Indian culture, but in fact the Lovers Rock scene was very much a Harlesden-based thing. The D in D. Tyrone appears to stand for either Don or David, depending on which website you believe, although given the number of pies he seemed to have had his fingers in, I'm inclined to think of him as some kind of mutant two-headed Dondavid / Davidon hydra-being. Either way, he seems to have eventually dropped the initial altogether, simply referring to himself as Tyrone. So that's what we shall do too from now on. Later on, we'll find out that his real name was something completely different, but we'll stick with Tyrone for the time being.

The first fruits of their collaboration would appear to be a 12" single on the JA-UK label, catalogue number PFU 2002, dated 1978. The A side is called 'Dennis The Menace' and the B side has the enticing name of 'Automatic Crystal Rankers'. Both tracks are credited to D. Pinnock ('Venture Music Pub. Co. Ltd.'), and the producer is credited as D. Tyrone, providing 'A

Gangster of Love Production'. Always nice to see the word gangster spelt correctly, by the way, although I guess this was back in the late 70s. The label itself looks a whole lot more professional than anything else that Dennis has been involved with so far, with all the copyright stuff that you'd usually expect to see there. So this was definitely a step up in the world.

The music is definitely a step up, too. There's a whole lot more going on in the accompaniment for one thing. Despite that, you can hear every word Dennis is singing: for the first time, he's in focus and it's great. This one zips along very nicely and you can tell he really wants it to be his signature record, and I can't help thinking it's a terrible shame that this one never made the crossover. Maybe he should have enlisted the help of the Beano and got them to change their Dennis' pullover from red and black stripes to red, gold and green for one issue. That's what I'd have done if I'd been his manager, anyway.

The record starts with a wacky sort of tape glitch effect, before launching into the backing track, over which Dennis hums along for a while before starting the song proper:

Give me a little time,
Please don't rush me
Let me swing
And do my thing

And so on. The chorus is a bit odd, though:

Automatic crystal remote control,
My name is Dennis the Menace,
Drop your soul.
Dennis is my name,
Music is my game,
Oh yeah.

I literally have no idea whatsoever as to what is going on in the first and third lines of that, but then again, I struggle with the likes of Bruce Springsteen's 'Blinded by the Light'. The only clue I could initially find was this line from Massive Attack's 'Risingson' (track number two on 1998's trip hop classic 'Mezzanine'):

Automatic crystal remote control,
We come to remove your soul

which also has a curious echo of Dennis' 'Drop your soul' line. However, if we explore the etymology a little further, it gets very complicated indeed.

The first reference to something like this line occurs in hip-hop pioneers The Last Poets' 'The Mean Machine' (from their 1971 album 'This Is Madness'). This track starts off with the following chant, repeated several times:

Automatic push-button remote control,
Synthetic genetics, control your soul

Fans of M|A|R|R|S may find this more than a little familiar, because they originally used a sample of it in 1987's 'Pump Up The Volume'. However, they were forced to change it for copyright reasons to the somewhat more meaningless:

Rhythmatic, systematic, world control,
Magnetic, genetic, dement your soul

(Love the word 'rhythmatic', incidentally. Should be used a lot more.)

The Dead Poets' phrase also became a favourite with reggae toasters such as Big Youth, although at some point it seems to have mutated into 'Automatic pistol remote control', once again leaving the original meaning some way behind in the dust.

Presumably Dennis Pinnock would have heard this as well, adding a further mutation of his own. Whether this was a simple case of mishearing or a deliberate change is lost in the mists of time, although the crystal reference is a little worrying, as it appears to carry a certain amount of hard drug baggage. Whatever the real reason, it's nice to think that Dennis' version of the phrase apparently somehow influenced a band as big as Massive Attack. Actually, it's more than nice. It's bloody gobsmacking, because that album regular gets placed on lists of the best albums of all time.

However, in the context of 'Dennis The Menace', the origin of the phrase scarcely matters, because as I say the overall effect is very pleasant indeed. Not only that, but there's over seven minutes' worth of it. Mr Tyrone clearly believed in giving value for money.

If we turn the record over, oh joy of joys, we have a genuine dub at last! 'Automatic Crystal Rankers' is a classic, over-the-top bonkers mangling of themes from 'Dennis the Menace', overlaid with wheeeees and burps from whatever cheap synths Tyrone happened to have lying around the studio. Dennis himself doesn't contribute much apart from one reprise of 'Dennis is my name' etc. and a half-hearted attempt at freestyle rapping towards the end, which doesn't really come off. But all the required components of dub are in there, including some nice crosscut echo.

I have to say that this one really should have been Dennis Pinnock's breakthrough disc. Signature song on one side, proper dub on the other, and ace production work from Tyrone. But again we are left to speculate as to what on earth went wrong. The other curiosity is what subsequently happened to the career of Tyrone himself. Clearly he was a highly competent producer, and one would have expected him to have gone onto great things as well. But perhaps he had too much on his hands, because it turns out that the JA-UK label was a subsidiary of Venture Records, of which Tyrone was the boss. So he was already dividing his time between running the label and managing his shop, and one can imagine that there probably wasn't an awful lot of space left over in his schedule.

The Revelation at Supertone Records

So much for social networking. After my Facebook and Myspace blitz, all I had to show for it after a couple of weeks of waiting patiently were a series of Myspace friend requests from total strangers who were desperate for me to listen to their tiresome twiddly music. So I broadened my reach by looking for the various people who Dennis had shared a disc with. Clearly Sugar Minott was a no-no, being dead, but I found the saxophonist Winston 'Saxton' Rose on Myspace and messaged him, again to no avail.

I also noticed that Janet Kay had an e-mail address on her website (even if it was unpromisingly given as info@janet-kay.com), so I got in touch with her, thus:

Hi Janet,

Hope you don't mind me getting in touch like this, but I'm a long time fan of the Lovers Rock scene [OK, I agree that was stretching it a bit – JP] who's researching a book and I really want to find out a bit more about Dennis Pinnock. I know your very first single (Loving You) had a version by him on the flipside and I wonder if you are still in touch with him, although I know it's a long time ago? Do you know if he is still alive and if he is at all contactable? I'd be really grateful for any information you could give me.

Many thanks in advance

However, either she hadn't actually spoken to the strange bloke who'd plastered Idi Amin all over the flipside of her first single, or she simply had a bad memory, because when she got back to me a week or so later, she claimed to have no knowledge of Dennis at all.

Hmmm. There was nothing for it. I was going to have to open up a second front. Maybe one of the independent record shops who'd sold me one of his records might be able to help? I've read *Hi Fidelity*: these places are crammed with geeks, aren't they? A quick scan of my archives revealed that the only real live bricks and mortar record shop I'd ordered anything from was Brixton's Supertone Records – and amazingly it seemed that they were still open for business in 2012. So I headed off to Acre Lane.

I used to know Brixton pretty well. The first ever flat I lived in was in Streatham, a few stops further south on the 159 bus, and my friends and I would often circulate around the area in between the two in search of a new place to drink. I also had a bit of a crush on a physiotherapist who I'd known for years and was living in Dalberg Road, which was – as they used to say in the days before the 1981 Brixton riots – a stone's throw from Coldharbour Lane. Despite the fact that her mum had had her eye on me as a potential son-in-law since we were at infants' school together, we were, for all my attentions, never more than just good friends.

She did at least provide an introduction to at least two of her housemates, neither of whom I succeeded in forming anything close to a relationship. This almost certainly would have had a considerable amount to do with my solid gold, precision-guaranteed ability to screw up any half-decent romantic opportunity thrown my way. I have learnt a lot since then, such as the all-important maxim that 'Apocalypse Now' is NOT a date movie. Neither for that matter is 'The Shining' or indeed 'Midnight Express', although I would say in mitigation that the last of these was the date's idea, not mine, so perhaps my choice of companion was also a bit iffy in those days.

In all the time since I'd last been there, Brixton hadn't actually changed that much. While parts of it were a bit smarter and parts of it were a bit seedier, the overall balance seemed to be pretty much the same as it always was. The streets were still thronging with as multicultural a crowd of folk as you'd wish to see in London. And, oh yes, some seriously well-stuffed woolly rasta hats.

The biggest change was that the old Little Bit Ritzy cinema had somehow mutated into the Ritzy Picturehouse complex with five screens. I wondered for a moment if they still did those all-night screenings of early John Waters' films. I do hope so; they were the very height of sleaze and unpleasantness. I have fond memories of the cheer that went up at 3am following *that* scene in 'Desperate Living'. You know, the one with the lesbian couple, the penis transplant and the scissors, right?

The other difference from the old Ritzy was that the selection of clingfilm-wrapped homemade cakes served at the box office seemed to have grown into a full-blown café serving very agreeable goat's-cheese-with-roasted-pepper-and-rocket ciabattas. So that was my white, middle-class lunch sorted, anyway, and afterwards I crossed over the road into Acre Lane in search of my goal.

It didn't take very long to find. Halfway along Acre Lane, there it was, opposite the Brixton branch of Lidl: Supertone Records. I hesitated on the threshold, worried about what I was going to say, afraid I was going to sound like some kind of lunatic. Then again, would it actually matter if I did? Brixton and I had managed quite happily without each other for nearly thirty years, so if I made a complete fool of myself now, I could probably get by without coming here for another thirty, by which time…

Oh, FFS.

I walked in the shop. It was small, but packed to the gills with vinyl and CDs. There was just me and an oldish, grey-haired chap who I took to be the proprietor in there. I'd decided that it might look a bit better if I actually bought something first before launching into my interrogation, so I started looking around vacantly.

'Are you looking for something?' he said with a genial expression on his face.

'Erm ... just browsing ... just browsing,' I replied, furiously scanning the shop for something to buy. The vinyl looked a bit scary and I felt I could easily make a telling mistake by asking for something banal and obvious instead of an obscure King Tubby dubplate (preferably the one with the inverted watermark on the label), so I stuck to the smaller and less intimidating selection of CDs by the door. Here at least were people I'd heard of, and I vacillated for several minutes between Gregory Isaacs and Lee 'Scratch' Perry before panicking completely and picking up a mundane Studio One ska compilation instead.

I handed it to the guy behind the counter, trying to ignore the warm sensation that was slowly creeping upwards from my neck.

'By the way,' I said, 'Do you know of a singer called Dennis Pinnock?'

An odd smile. 'Yes,' he said, 'I know him.'

Dignity PLC

For the purposes of introducing a bit of shameless narrative excitement, we're going to leave the search for Dennis poised on that cliffhanger and take a quick detour to Somerset, in search of the Pinnock family grave. Locating Portishead Cemetery turned out to be more than a little problematic. Most of the references on Google appeared to point to an address in Weston-Super-Mare, so that's what I tapped into the SatNav. Unfortunately, when we were getting quite close, the SatNav lady decided to direct me into a dead end in the middle of an out-of-town shopping precinct. Cursing her under my breath, I did a three-point turn, whereupon she proceeded to direct me, without a single word of apology, back out of the shopping precinct in the right direction this time.

However, once she took me to the graveyard in question, it became all too apparent that it was not the one I was looking for. I'd been expecting something a bit like Highgate, but this place was like the result of an encounter between a tornado and a trailer park. I swear there were pink flamingos decorating at least one of the graves, and whoever had the idea of implanting photographic portraits in the headstones needs to be locked up for a very long time and subjected to a strict regime of radical re-education. I felt I had now seen the twenty-first century way of death and it was using *Take a Break* as its style guide. The icing on the cake was that the running of the cemetery and its associated crematorium seemed to have been handed over to a company called Dignity PLC. One day I'll go back there and have a hunt for the final resting place of Satire; it's got to be in there somewhere.

After consulting Google again, I managed to find the original

Portishead cemetery, conveniently situated this time in Portishead. I'm convinced the SatNav lady gave a bit of a sigh when we arrived, as if to say, well this is nice: a lovely sunny weekend morning in spring, and all we end up doing is exploring graveyards. She got her revenge later on that day by sending me into a bus lane in Bath, resulting in a thirty quid fine. Our relationship hasn't been quite the same since.

Portishead cemetery turned out to be a much more sober affair with mostly good, solid, traditional headstones with only the occasional Bart Simpson figurine to break the spell. What it was lacking, however, was any sort of map that would help me pin down where Section L Number 68 might be found. There was nothing for it but to scour the entire graveyard.

Fortunately, Portishead is not a particularly big cemetery and it was also quite easy to discard a large proportion of the graves because they were clearly quite recent. However, that still left quite a few to check out, and the inscriptions on several of them were very hard to decipher. One or two unfortunate ones actually had trees growing through the middle of them, which I guess at least suggested that some useful recycling had probably taken place. Even where the headstones were still intact, the local authority, who still seemed to be running this one – Dignity PLC presumably being uninterested in what I'd really love to think would be referred to as 'legacy sites' – had knocked a fair number of them over, presumably for misplaced fear of health and safety litigation.

After half an hour or so of fruitless searching, I was on the point of giving up when I arrived at the very last area to be examined. And there it was. Three foot high and still standing proud, the headstone that marked the Pinnock family grave:

JOSEPH BROWN PINNOCK
OF PORTISHEAD
DEPARTED THIS LIFE 9TH AUGUST 1916
IN THE 65TH YEAR OF HIS AGE

MARY JANE PINNOCK
DEPARTED THIS LIFE 9TH FEBRUARY 1930
IN THE 74TH YEAR OF HER AGE

And that was it. No bollocks about going to sleep or finding peace in the arms of Jesus: just the bald facts. I was beginning to warm to my great-grandparents.

However, for all that, the grave wasn't actually telling me anything more than I knew already. Indeed, there didn't seem to be any mention at all of the other two occupants mentioned in the e-mail: my Great Uncle Harry and Great Aunt Mary. So if I wanted to get any further with my own ancestry, I was going to have to go back to that box of papers after all.

As I was leaving the cemetery, I passed by the grave of an eight-year-old boy who had died in 2001. It was relatively tasteful and spotlessly clean with a couple of well-watered tubs of plants, and I wondered about what it must be like for his parents, more than ten years on, still coming here every week to tend to his site. And then I felt bad about thinking up cheap gags about tornados and trailer parks. Well, for a moment I did. Then I thought, sod it. You deal with it your way, I'll deal with it mine. Death is a pretty damn confusing business, but it's nothing if not personal.

Gangster of Love

Dennis Pinnock's time working with Tyrone is reasonably well documented, mainly due to a page on the Songcast MP3 distribution web site devoted to 'BLRM Records', although – as we shall shortly see – we should perhaps be wary of taking everything there at face value. BLRM stands for 'British Lovers Rock Music', and would seem to be a recent vehicle set up to re-market tracks from the Venture label as MP3 downloads, although the only one available on that site at the time of writing is Eargasm's 'This Is Lovers Rock', of which more in a later chapter.

The biography given for Tyrone makes some pretty extravagant claims, starting with his description as 'producer, singer, songwriter, arranger and multi-instrumentalist, entrepreneur and chef' before going on to state that he was a founder-member of Aswad alongside Brinsley Forde. Well, I don't feel in a position to dispute his talents as a chef (although it does seem a tad gratuitous to mention them in his bio), but I can't find any corroborative reference to Tyrone whatsoever in the context of Aswad. His bio goes on to claim that he discovered 'Frenchi King, Black Stallion, Tradition, Janet Kay, Tim Chandelle, Paulette Walker, Elements, Snoopy, Dennis Pinnock, Lamour, Investigators, Aurora York, Steven (JLC).' Not only that, but he also 'inspired, mentored, promoted and marketed ... Tex Johnson, Alton Ellis, Dixie Peach, Hortense Ellis, Owen Gray, Lindel Lewis, Gene Rondo, Norman J Star Collins, Delroy Wilson, Junior English, Ronney Davis, Winston Reedy, Paula Clarke, Jah Stich, Sugar Minott, Pliers, Johnny

Waler, George Faith, Chuck Turner, Purple Man, Hugh Griffiths, Pinchers, Peaches, Tony Rebel & Bimbo, Don Angelo, Skanie 1, Frankie Wilmott, Klassique and many others.'

Wow. I think it's the 'and many others' that's the real killer there. Maybe he really did inspire, mentor, promote and market all those folk (including some pretty big names, as you can see), although I can't help feeling that he'd at least have his own Wikipedia entry if that were truly the case. There's some stuff about Dennis Pinnock on the same page, including the fascinating information that he was originally from Peckham. Crikey, he could have been living in the next street when I was there. The note also says that Tyrone has recorded an album with Dennis to be called 'Dennis the Menace', adding that this has not yet been released. It concludes by saying that Dennis Pinnock is a great talent and a name to watch out for.

I'm guessing the text on this page must have been taken from some kind of Venture Records press release from back in the 80s, given that the promise of that album is still waiting to be fulfilled. Anyway, the good news is that it also gives a list of the records that he worked with Tyrone on, and the first of these is called 'Ride On'.

'Ride On' is a 12" single on the Venture label, catalogue number VNLP92 (1978). The song is credited to Dennis Pinnock, and production is by D. Tyrone. The label design is green with a yellow five-pointed star superimposed on it. On top of this there is a rather arresting pen and ink drawing of a dapper chap in a three-piece pinstripe suit and trilby hat lassoing a well-dressed and ample-bosomed young lady around the neck. The lady is carrying a feather boa, which I think is an especially nice touch. The words 'A GANGSTER OF LOVE PRODUCTION' are written along the length of the lasso. You may be relieved to know that Venture only used this design for their first few releases, before switching to a considerably duller, albeit somewhat less sexist, cloud-based design.

The B side of 'Ride On' is called 'Rock On', and the writing is again credited to Dennis Pinnock. However, it's actually performed by a group called Tradition, another bunch who – do please stop me if you've heard this one before – went on to greater things. Tradition actually signed to big boys RCA for a brief period and produced a number of well-received albums. However, at the time of this recording, in 1978, they were just on the cusp of their breakthrough and still recording with Tyrone as his house band.

'Ride On' / 'Rock On' rather excitingly has a picture sleeve, although I only know this because it turned up when I ordered an entirely different Dennis Pinnock single via eBay. And truth to tell, it isn't actually that brilliant, consisting as it does of a simple blue and white graphic design of a chap in a helmet riding a motorbike. Not only that, but Dennis' surname (my surname too, damn it) is spelt as 'Pinock'. So one house point to be deducted from the designer, A. Nero, I think.

The song itself starts in a very similar manner to 'Dennis the Menace', with a brief intro followed by a spell of Dennis vocalising over a backing track (provided, one assumes, by Tradition). And then the lyric starts:

A knife and a fork,
A bottle and a cork,
That's the way we spell New York

Now, stop right there, Mr P. Isn't that a direct, unattributed lift from Dillinger's 1976 classic 'Cocaine in my Brain'? Admittedly, there's a lot more to the Dillinger song than just that one refrain, but then again, it does constitute over 50% of the lyrics of 'Ride on'. However, we'll give him the benefit of the doubt for now and look at the rest of the record. This first verse is followed by a whole series of repeats of the phrase 'Ride on, ride on', and then the second verse comes in:

We dance and we sing
We dance and we swing,
That's the way we do our thing

and so on, with more 'Ride on, ride ons' followed by a reprise of the first verse. There's actually a really nice lilting feel to this record, which I guess we can put down to Tradition's backing, and it must have been great to dance to, so we can probably forgive Dennis his borrowing of Dillinger's line.

Flipping the record over, 'Rock On' turns out to be a rather spiffy dub version of 'Ride On', so it's still Dennis' record really, given that Tradition were effectively his backing band. However, I guess their star was in the ascendant so they got the credit. Good luck to them.

According to the DanceCrasher web site, this single actually reached number nine in the pre-release 12" reggae charts in *Black Music* magazine in January 1978, the only time that Dennis actually made a solo appearance as far as I can tell. It is another excellent record to add to the Pinnock canon. And indeed the Pinock one for that matter.

Where Wallie Was

Back in Brixton, my brain had lurched into a frantic ducking and diving manoeuvre in a vain attempt to block the curveball that had just been hurled in its direction.

'You ... know him?' I gasped.

'Yeah.'

'He's still alive, then?'

'Yeah. He's a local boy.'

'He lives in Brixton?'

'Yeah. Other end.' He waved vaguely back down Acre Lane.

'Gosh. You see,' I gabbled, 'I've always been interested in him, because my ... um ... name's Pinnock too.'

Another odd smile. Yes, the man in your shop is a lunatic. But he seems harmless, and he's just paid you way over the odds for a ska compilation he could have picked up on Amazon for half the price.

'Does he still sing?'

He smiled again and shook his head. 'I don't think so.'

'Would it be possible for me to speak to him?'

Another shake of the head. 'Maybe. But I don't have his number.'

Ah. So close and yet so far. Still, I gave him my card in case he remembered anything or if the man himself happened to drop in. I asked him his name, and he said he was called Wallie. So at least I now knew where Wallie was, even if the bigger question, 'Where's Dennis?' was yet to be answered.

'Look at my website!' he called after me as I left.

'I will!' I replied. It's *www.supertonerecords.co.uk* in case you were wondering, and very good it is too.

This was the best progress I'd made so far. I now knew that not only was Dennis Pinnock alive, but he was living in Brixton. On a whim, I nipped into the library next to the Ritzy and went in search of the local telephone directory. I should have realised. The one directory out of the whole country that was missing was the one containing the numbers for London SW2. I would either have to go to a library somewhere away from Brixton or look on the internet. So that was that for now.

It was a sunny afternoon and I was footloose and fancy-free, so I thought I'd go and take a look at Peckham for old times' sake while I was in the vicinity. Ignoring the old Thatcherite adage that anyone over the age of 30 who finds himself on a bus can be considered a failure, I hopped onto the number 37 to Peckham Rye, taking in the view from the front of the top deck as it followed the weird London switchback between affluence and destitution as one street turned into another.

Amazingly, my old house in Bellenden Road looked exactly the same, at least from the outside. To all intents and purposes, it had neither gone down in the world nor – as far as I could tell – gone up much. The *Il Giardino* pizza restaurant across the road from the railway station was still there, although it was no longer in competition with the frankly pretty unpleasant eel pie and mash place that used to squat opposite to it. The Albert pub across the road was also still around, the sole change being the inevitable addition of Sky Sports to the list of attractions.

To be fair, there were also a few signs of upward movement to go along with that insane twenty-fivefold increase in house prices. There were a few new restaurants, for example, as well as – quite unbelievably – a tiny independent bookshop. I felt obliged to buy something because it looked like I was going to be their only customer that day, with the result that I spent the journey home being alternately impressed and infuriated by a particular short story collection that was supposed to be a lot better than it actually was. But the junk shop where I'd originally bought 'Take It Cool' was sadly long gone, replaced by an upmarket deli.

When I got back home I reflected that my first day of research out in the field instead of sitting at a computer terminal had actually gone pretty well. I had progressed from a position of knowing absolutely nothing about my target's whereabouts to pinning him down to a specific postcode district in London. I really couldn't have asked for more than that. Maybe it was true what they all said about me. I did need to get out a bit more.

Oh, and that ska CD wasn't that bad either. It had – inevitably – several tracks on it by The Skatalites (but then they are pretty reliable), alongside an unusual early tune by none other than The Maytals (pre-Toots, presumably) called 'Marching On', which turned out to be based on 'When the Saints Go Marching In'. There was also a piece by The Ethiopians, who I hadn't heard of before, although I was familiar with The Abyssinians. I wondered if they ever shared a platform, and if so, did The Abyssinians feel they had some kind of prior claim over the territory? Tricky business, names.

Dog-Face Phil

It was time to follow up the Jamaican connection. The last we heard was that in 1773, a Philip Pinnock and a James Pinnock were acting as shipping agents on the island, as evidenced by Samuel Munckley of Bristol's bill of lading. People like them must have had a pivotal role in the transatlantic trade, given that they were the ones who handled everything from sorting out a berth for the incoming vessel to arranging for the cargo to be loaded. Samuel Munckley, on the other hand, was a hot-shot ship owner and merchant based in Bristol whose name turns up on a whole swathe of documents relating to the Jamaican route, although only one of them seems to involve Messrs Pinnock. Maybe they tried to rip him off, or perhaps they were just incompetent.

The first decision I had to make was whether to go after Philip or James first, so I tossed a coin and Philip won. It wasn't that hard in the end to track down Philip Pinnock, at least once I'd shelled out for a subscription to the Ancestry website and banged his name into the search box, along with Jamaica as the location and 1700-ish as his date of birth. One of the first references popped up in the Kingston *Daily Gleaner*, which I was particularly pleased about because the *Daily Gleaner* has long been my second-favourite name for a newspaper. My all-time favourite is the *Sacramento Bee*, and it's my firm opinion that if there were more Bees and Gleaners and fewer, say, Timeses, the world would almost certainly be a much happier place.

Even better, the *Daily Gleaner* from December 11th, 1944 has a picture of a Philip Pinnock, although the quality of the reproduction leaves a little to be desired and we'll have to take the word of the editorial team that it is indeed a portrait of a real person and not in fact the head of a slightly pissed-off Alsatian dog.

This Philip Pinnock apparently lived from 1720 to 1778, which puts him right in the frame for being the one who was in communication with Mr Munckley in 1773. Intriguingly, the guy in the picture in the *Daily Gleaner* was apparently Speaker of the House of Assembly as well as being Custos of the parish of St Andrew – in fact this is the reason for his appearance in the paper, because the article is about 'The Powers & Functions Of The Speaker' and relates to the proposed reintroduction of such an office. In case you're wondering, Custos is short for 'Custos Rotolorum', which is Latin for 'keeper of the rolls' – in other words, the first citizen of the parish, responsible for the maintenance of good order and discipline in the parish and upholding the rule of law. So he was clearly a man of some significance.

Precisely why an ancient portrait of Philip Pinnock (captioned 'A SPEAKER OF THE PAST') was chosen to illustrate this article was unclear. One could only imagine he was a particularly famous (or, tantalisingly, notorious) holder of the position. Given this, we can probably assume that he was of some stature in Jamaica, which would also mean that he was almost certainly a man of some wealth and hence a landowner. 'Land' in the context of Jamaica would have almost certainly meant 'plantation', so it was now pretty much inevitable that Philip was also a major league slave owner. I was already going off him when I first saw his canine portrait, but he was definitely off my Christmas card list now. I was also beginning to wonder if such an exalted person would also be working as a shipping agent.

A bit more digging, this time on the excellent Jamaican Family Search website, turned up some further information about the same chap, in an article by one F. J. duQuesnay, reproduced from the *Daily Gleaner* of March 31st, 1965, under the curious heading 'Philip Pinnock, the dandy'. Now I have to say my spirits perked up considerably when I read this, as there is no possible way that I could share a single segment of my DNA with someone who went under the soubriquet of 'The Dandy'. I am most definitely not a dandy: my dress sense is vanishingly small. There are strange unmentionable lifeforms eking out an existence at the bottom of the Mariana Trench that have better dress sense than I have.

But there it was: 'Philip Pinnock, the dandy', and duQuesnay's article goes on to say that somewhere there exists a portrait of him – reputedly by Allan Ramsay, court painter to King George III – in which:

> *he wears a wig, and deep blue velvet coat elaborately embroidered in gold. Lace ruffles fall about his wrists and beneath his left arm he holds a cocked-hat.*

Lovely. The piece fails to mention that Pinnock also had the face of a dog, but I guess that might have broken the spell.

duQuesney provides a few more dates relating to the Pinnock family, although we should perhaps treat them with a little circumspection as he has Philip Pinnock dying in 1773, five years before The *Daily Gleaner*'s date. Either way, it seems that the Pinnocks were there pretty much right from the start of the Jamaican occupation. The island was taken by the English in 1655 and less than forty years later, in 1691, James Pinnock, son of James and Ann, was christened in the St Andrew Parish church at Halfway Tree. James Junior subsequently married Elizabeth, who gave birth to Dog-Face Phil.

But was he the same guy as the Philip Pinnock I'd originally been looking for? And if he was the same guy, who was the

James Pinnock mentioned along with him on that bill of lading? Philip's father was certainly a James Pinnock, but he would have been long dead in 1773, and his only son was called either Dakin (if you take F. J. duQuesnay's spelling) or Dawkins (if you go with a more thorough genealogy produced by John Stuart-Russell, of whom more anon). Either way, the poor kid died at the age of three, long before he would have completed his shipping agency training.

No, it's much more likely that the Philip and James Pinnock referred to on Samuel Munckley's bill of lading came from another branch of the family, which would almost certainly make them Dog-Face Phil's nephews. This information comes from a very comprehensive family tree prepared by the aforementioned John Stuart-Russell and provided to Jamaican Family Search by P. Dowling, who provides the most extraordinary background note, as follows:

The information I sent concerning the Pinnock Family was created using a Pedigree Chart provided by my late cousin John Stuart-Russell, who prepared the chart in 1911. Regrettably most of the source material was destroyed when the family had to flee Eastern Papua in 1942 when the Japanese bombed the island and destroyed the family home.

A damn shame that, but understandable in the circumstances. However, in the end I had to leave Mr Stuart-Russell and his unfortunate family behind now because their fate was, sadly, irrelevant to my present search, grateful though I was for the man's genealogical work. Neither did it actually matter that quite by chance I seemed to have located an entirely different Philip Pinnock from the one I had originally been looking for. The important thing is that, one way or another, I had somehow stumbled on the man who, as far as eighteenth-century Jamaica was concerned, was the über-Pinnock, the pinnacle of the Pinnocks: Philip Pinnock, 1720 to 1778. As we shall see in due course, he was a man of quite some significance.

Take It Cool

Dennis Pinnock's third record with Tyrone, and his second on the Venture label is 1978's 7" disc 'Take It Cool', catalogue number OWN 1. This is the record that started this whole weird journey off. The dubious pin-stripe-bloke-lassoing-a-floozy label design of the 'Ride On'-era Venture has thankfully been dropped in favour of three stylised white clouds on a sky-blue background, with a yellow sun peeking out of the largest one. There's a discreet hint of novelty on the label, too, with the A side referred to as the 'Top Side' and the B side referred to as the 'Bottom Side'. The B side has the ever-brilliant title of 'Pinnock's Paranormal Payback'. Both tracks are credited to D.Pinnock/Tyrone, and Tyrone also takes the production credits on the both sides, although 'Pinnock's Paranormal Payback'* is 'arranged and mixed by The Gruesome Twosome'. No idea who the Gruesome Twosome are, although my money's on Pinnock and Tyrone themselves.

'Take It Cool' has a slight variation on the standard Tyrone/Pinnock template, although it starts with the usual flourish from the backing band followed by wordless vocalising. However, this time there's also a backing chorus that comes in first:

---

* As we'll see later, Tyrone has a bit of a penchant for wordplay. The B side of his own single 'Too Late to Turn Back Now' has the equally brilliant title 'Tyrone's Transcendental Twist.'

I tell it to the East
And I tell it to the West
I tell it to the North
And I tell it to the South

It isn't clear who's doing the backing vocals – it could well be a multi-tracked Pinnock himself or Tyrone and some of his mates – but it's all very nicely sung in close harmony.

After a while, Pinnock starts the song proper:

Serious time,
Now a serious time,
Serious time,
Now a serious time,
Take it cool, natty,
Serious time,
Take it cool, dready,
Serious time,

and so on. It then gets a bit difficult to follow, but the essence seems to be that bad times are just around the corner, so watch out and stay cool. It's worth remembering that these were nervous, jumpy times with support for the National Front at its highest level and the post-war liberal consensus preparing to implode in the 1979 general election.

Long-time reggae fans will notice that favourite word 'natty' there and if, like me, you went out and bought a copy of Bob Marley and the Wailers' breakthrough album 'Natty Dread' without having a clue what the title meant, it's about time we found out, right? The only problem is that, not for the first time, the internet does not speak with one voice on the subject. Depending on which website you pick, it seems that on its own, 'natty' can either mean 'natural', 'knotty' or any number of variants of 'cool'. However, in the context of the lyrics of 'Take It Cool', it's perhaps best to take it as shorthand for 'Natty Dread', which describes a member of the Rastafarian community, identified by his natural/knotted dreadlocks.* Oddly, the word 'dready' does not exist at all, and would appear to have been made up by Dennis Pinnock in order to (a) complete the stock 'natty dread' phrase but (b) without breaking the rhythm. Still, we can sort of see what he means.

Tyrone's production is exemplary as ever and the backing track jogs along in the manner we've come to expect, although there is perhaps a little too much of one particular synthesized beeping noise that last saw use in a contemporary arcade game such as 'Space Invaders' or 'Pong'. The real revelation of 'Take It Cool', however, is in the close-harmony vocals – a pointer perhaps to Dennis' future work as part of Eargasm and Four In A Row.

On the Bottom Side, '**Pinnock's Paranormal Payback**' is a well-executed although not particularly OTT dub of 'Take It Cool', although with a bit more of the space invaders. And that would be that, except...

We have a bonus! Not long afterwards, 'Take It Cool' was re-released as a 12", catalogue number EAR 16, with 'Dennis The Menace' on the Bottom Side this time. Even better than that, there's also a version on TRANSPARENT GREY VINYL! Everyone was doing this kind of thing in the late 70s. I remember buying a Lavender-coloured copy of Squeeze's ballad 'Up The Junction', although the way in which the specific colour connected Clapham Junction and Lavender Hill was more than a little tenuous. What made it cool for me was that I actually bought it from a record shop on Lavender Hill, just round the corner from where I was living at the time.

I have to say, however, that transparent grey is not an arresting colour for a single and to be honest it just looks as if it's

---

* Incidentally, the fact that both natural and knotted fit the meaning of 'natty' in this context suggests to the amateur linguist in me that the derivation has actually been retrofitted to the word and not the other way around.

been left out in the sun for a bit too long. Never mind. 'Take It Cool' still sounds good, and you get an even longer mix of it for your money – 5 minutes 35 seconds as opposed to 2 minutes 51 seconds. 'Dennis the Menace' is, however, slightly shorter than the previous monster, clocking in at 5 minutes 52 seconds instead of 7 minutes 9 seconds. I'm pretty certain that Pinnock's vocal track is exactly the same, although the production seems a fair bit smoother, albeit with the unnecessary addition of some cowbell.

The good thing about listening to this again is that it still sounds as fresh as it did all those years ago. What's interesting to me, in the context of the rest of Dennis Pinnock's career, is spotting the pointers as to what happened next. And I know I keep saying this, but with every single one of these recordings, I wonder what it was that stopped him from breaking through into the big time. This is seriously good stuff, you know. It really is.

Round about this time, Dennis was also briefly involved in a side project, the duo 'Dennis & Lauraine'. Lauraine turns out to be Lauraine Smart, subsequently also known as Lorraine McIntosh, wife of Steve and father of Bradley. Yes, Bradley McIntosh from S Club 7. You can stop squealing now, kids. Lorraine had a very successful career herself, alongside hubby Steve in The Cool Notes, who spent the seventies as a reggae band before switching to soul in the eighties, scoring several hits – including most memorably the disco smash 'Spend the Night', which got to number 11 in 1985.

Dennis & Lauraine's only record is called 'You and Me Baby' on the Soferno B label. Soferno B ran one of the top sound systems in South London at the time, occasionally diversifying into record production as well. Interestingly, according to the biographical note about Dennis on the BLRM page on the Songcast website that we first came across in the 'Gangster of Love' chapter, Tyrone is recorded as first encountering him when he was DJ-ing for *Soprano* B. A little digging reveals that Soprano

B was just another name that Soferno B went under, so he and Dennis clearly had a fairly long-standing relationship. According to the label, 'You and Me Baby' is arranged by L. Matador and produced by Soferno B, with a writing credit to C. Mayfield. This immediately suggested that it was a cover of a song by the late soul titan Curtis Mayfield, although it took a little longer than expected to track down as it turns out that it's actually called 'Between You Baby and Me'. Mayfield's version, incidentally, is on his 1979 album 'Heartbeat', where he duets with Linda Clifford.

Dennis & Lauraine's version sensibly omits the cheesy spoken-word intro that blights the original, and substitutes a lightly up-tempo reggae beat for Mayfield's slow and smoochy waltz. Both singers acquit themselves well – especially Lauraine, who is more than a match for her soul counterpart – and it's interesting to see Dennis using the material to stretch his voice towards a more soulful delivery. The backing track is a little thin, and it's left particularly exposed on the B side, 'You and Me Dub'. This is a forgettable dub with hardly any vocals at all, credited to 'Soferno B Rhythm Rulers'. Still, the A side is pleasant enough, even if it is more than a little poignant to see Dennis working with yet another artist who went on to much better things.

Nailors and Nob Thatchers

Having established that there were no further clues to Joseph Brown Pinnock (I) from the family grave, I went back to my father's box of papers. There I came across a brief memoir written by my grandfather, a lovely guy who went by the name of Archibald Robert Pinnock, although everyone referred to him as 'Pop'.

In Pop's memoir, he describes how his father went to Canada in 1871 and stayed there for five years, originally staying with his cousin, a farmer. As Pop says, 'I don't think he took to farming for he seems to have tried many things. I don't think he made a fortune at any of them!' Back in the UK, however, he seems to have made a decent living for himself as the bookkeeper at the Bristol Galvanised Iron company amongst other places – enough certainly to have bought himself a substantial burial plot. I also have a humungously large photographic portrait of him – the frame is almost three foot by two and a half, so he was clearly a man with an eye on posterity.

Unfortunately, he left behind precious little in the way of pointers as to his ancestry, and for some reason my father and uncle both seem to have focused their efforts on his wife's side of the tree and not his own. His wife was born Mary Jane Collins, and she came into the world in 1856. Her early life cannot have been easy because her mother died before she reached the age of three; I know this because the box of papers contains a photocopy of the marriage certificate for her father and her stepmother, which took place in 1859. Her father, Henry Collins, lists his profession as 'puddler', which from the sound of it was a highly skilled but deeply scary job, involving a reverbatory furnace and an awful lot of molten iron.

However, this wasn't getting me any further back up the Pinnock tree, so I put the Collinses to one side and returned to Joseph Brown (I), starting with the UK census records. 1901 found him unexpectedly in Dover, listed as 'Traveller' and staying at The Temperance Hotel in Strond Street, which sounds like a jolly establishment. The rest of the family, meanwhile, were back in Salthorp Road, Bristol, where my grandfather, aged 15, was excitingly described as a laboratory assistant. I'm quite envious of this, because my parents never let me have a chemistry set, however hard I pestered them. Going back a bit further, in 1891, the whole family were all together in Stackpool Road in the Bedminster district of Bristol, where JBP is listed as an accountant in manufacturing. They also seem to have a 14-year-old domestic servant in the shape of Helena Saunders, so things must have been going pretty well – although I guess 14-year-old girls came quite cheap in those days.

In 1881, Joseph and Mary Pinnock, three years into their marriage, were living with their infant first-born son, Jesus – sorry, Harry – in Bradley Lane, Sedgley, Wolverhampton, along with 15-year-old domestic servant Mary Ann Langston. Joseph was employed as a clerk at the iron works and Mary as a schoolmistress. But hold on, we seem to have moved away from Bristol towards the Midlands. Indeed, in 1871, young 19-year-old Joseph is living with his folk down the road in Tipton – presumably just before his Canadian adventure. At this time he seems to have been working as a clerk at the local colliery. His parents are John and Harriet. John is described as an 'agent', which is almost certainly much less exciting than it sounds.

In 1861, the family are still in Tipton, and in fact they don't seem to have moved very far in the preceding half-century, because as we shall see shortly, on John Pinnock's birth certificate, the location is listed as Dudley – right next door. At this time, John Pinnock is still working as an 'agent', although back in 1851 he's a mere 'machine keeper'. Also in the house on this occasion is his niece Hestor, who at the age of 13 is working as a 'nailor'. I had to look this up and found an excellent site describing old occupations, which told me that – duh – a nailor was someone who made iron nails by hand. However, I must report that my inner twelve-year-old was way more excited to find out on the same page that the old name for someone who made wigs was a 'nob thatcher'. That's real history, that is. And all I can say is that if you resisted the urge to shout out the word 'merkin', you're a better man than I am.

Going back to 1841, the earliest available census record, John Pinnock is also working – in common with pretty much everyone in Snow Hill, Dudley, it seems – as a nailor. Dudley must have been the nail capital of the world in those days, although these days, you'd be more likely to find a nail parlour than anywhere where nails are actually being manufactured. However, there weren't any hints in the record as to John's parentage as he was already 25 years old and appeared to be sharing accommodation with some bloke called John Saddler, aged 55.

I did find a couple of other clues, however. A John Pinnock from Dudley got married in 1840, according to the index of births, marriages and deaths transcribed by the excellent FreeBMD project. Disappointingly, there were no clues as to the name of the bride, so it was by no means certain that this was the same John Pinnock. Certainly, her absence from his side – indeed, the apparent absence of anyone answering to the name of Harriet Pinnock or anything like it – at the time of the 1841 census was troubling. However, three Harriets did get married in Dudley during that quarter, so it was by no means inconceivable that one of them got hitched to our John. It was clear that the only way I was going to resolve this was by sending off for a copy of the marriage certificate itself, so that's what I did.

The other clue was the registration of birth for a John Pinnock in Dudley in 1815, which fitted the age recorded in the census records. But I had to find this by transferring my attentions to *familysearch.org*, which meant I was now in the realm of the Church of Jesus Christ of Latter-Day Saints. One of the more bizarre aspects of genealogical research is that if you dig deep enough, there comes a point where you end up having to make use of the vast database being compiled by the Genealogical Society of Utah, which is essentially the genealogical wing of the Mormons.

As I understand it, the thinking behind this massive and, presumably, horrendously expensive effort is in order to assist the prophet Elijah to bind families together for eternity when he eventually shows up again. Which is nice, except my feeling at this point in my research was that if I did indeed turn out to be related to Dog-Face Phil of Jamaica, I would have much preferred it if I could spend eternity without him breathing down my neck. Believe me, I've had a few dodgy family Christmases and the thought of spending for ever and ever amen with a whole bunch of Pinnocks wasn't necessarily an attractive proposition.

Anyway, the available information about this John Pinnock's birth gave his father as another John Pinnock and his mother as Frances. At this point I really would have preferred something a bit more unusual and searchable, like Octavian and Chardonnay, but I guess I'd have to make do with boring old Johnny and Franny. However, I was still going to need a few more pointers, so I needed an image of the actual birth record – although I had no idea as to whether this would indeed yield any further clues.

It turned out that all I had to do was pay a nominal rental fee for the microfiche containing the image I was looking for. I was initially worried that, having signed up for an account, I would be opening myself up to visits by pairs of strangely clean cut young men with perfect white teeth and unconventional underwear. So for a time I took to keeping a gimp mask by the door in order to scare them off in the event that they came to call. My next – more practical – concern, that I didn't possess a microfiche reader myself, was allayed by the fact that this microfiche would be delivered to a designated 'FamilySearch Center'. For a brief moment I was worried that I would need to travel to Salt Lake City and spend a week enjoying the pleasures of abstinence, but it was worse than that.

I would have to go to Stevenage.

Doorstep Delivery

Having failed to locate the local phone directory when I was actually in Brixton, I tried online. But this wasn't any more use in tracking Dennis Pinnock down: there were only four Pinnocks listed in Brixton with landlines, and none of them had the initial D. The next line of attack was the electoral roll, so I paid £4.50 to Peopletracer, for which princely sum I got five shots at pinning the man down.

First of all, I tried searching for all the Pinnocks in SW2. There were, impressively, thirty of the buggers, but once again there wasn't a single Dennis. Then I widened the search to next-door SE24 and a further seven Pinnocks turned up. But still no joy. In desperation, I simply changed the search to find all Dennis Pinnocks in London. There were four, and joy of joys, one of them lived in one of the other postal districts adjoining SW2 – not only that, but it was indeed in the vague direction that Wallie of Supertone Records had pointed. This had to be him. However, there was a problem: he was only listed on the electoral register up to 2003. Had he moved on, or had he simply accidentally disenfranchised himself? I had two searches left. This time I put in his postcode, but left the name blank. There were no more names subsequently registered on the electoral roll, so I was pretty damn sure this had to be him.

The next question was how to make the approach. I could, I guess, have simply knocked on his door, although the chances of that working out well were, I felt, fairly minimal. How would the conversation go? What if, for example, his wife or some other member of his family happened to answer the door?

'Er … Hello. Is Dennis in?'

'Yeah. What do you want?'

'Well, I'm … I'm writing a book about him.'

[Incredulous] 'You what?'

'I'm … writing a book – '

[Shakes head] 'Yeah, I heard. You need help, man.'

'No, honestly. It's really interesting. It's about slavery and stuff too. I'm reviewing all his records in it. I'm a big fan.'

'Man, you really do need help.'

[Smacks head] 'No, you see, I forgot to say. My name's Pinnock, too.'

[Shakes head again] 'Stay there. I'll call him. DENNIS! Funny-looking bloke with a beard says he's writing a book about you.'

[Sound of uncontrollable laughter]

[Apologetic smile] 'Sorry, man. Just leave us alone, will you?'

'Can I leave my – ' [Door closes in face]

It would probably have been even worse if Dennis himself had answered the door. I would simply have stammered for a moment before turning tail and fleeing. As I said back at the start, I'm pretty inept at dealing with people in real life, even when I've got a simple message to get across, such as 'a white sandwich and half a dozen granary baps, please'. A complex message like this one would be almost impossible to get across on a potentially hostile doorstep; I would have to write a letter instead. But what guarantee did I have that he'd reply? The answer was that there was no guarantee whatsoever. Then again, if he didn't reply, I could at least doorstep him and say I was following up my earlier correspondence, couldn't I? Yeah. No problem. No problem at all.

The next question was what on earth should I say in the letter. I wasn't even sure how to start it.

Hi Dennis,

No. This is not an e-mail, you idiot. Try again.

Dear Dennis,

Too chummy. Remember, he's your generation. You like to be called by your surnames by strangers, right?

Dear Mr Pinnock,

No, no no! It's not a frigging council tax demand!

Dear Dennis Pinnock,

OK, that'll do. Now what?

I have been following your career with interest.

Nope. Too formal. Also, it's actually a bit creepy.

Greetings in the name of Jah, Ras Dennis!

Oh, FFS. Who am I kidding?

I'm a writer.

Well, it's a bit better than starting by announcing that I molest small children, but not a lot better.

I'm writing a book about you.

Oh, good grief. That's just plain weird.

I wonder if you can help me. I'm writing a book about the name Pinnock and how it came to cross the race boundary, amongst other things. It's a very interesting tale, as you may know already.

OK, not quite the whole story but maybe we'll keep that for an opening. And?

I was actually inspired to write this by coming across one of your records back in the 80s and I've actually collected all the others in the years since. ~~I'm a particular fan of your work with Tyrone.~~

Careful. We don't yet know if he's still on speakies with Tyrone.

I'm planning to write about this in the book as well.

OK, now that should grab his attention.

What I'd really like to do is meet with you some time and chat about your career. Would you be happy to be interviewed for the book?

That'll do. Keep it short and sweet. I added my contact details and sent it off. It was almost an entire day later that I realised that I'd completely forgotten to ask the most important question in the letter:

You ARE the same Dennis Pinnock, aren't you?

Hmmm. This could yet go horribly wrong.

The Harlesden Sound

Dennis Pinnock's third collaboration with Tyrone is called 'I've Only Just Begun' (Venture Records, 1980, catalogue number EAR 25). However, on the label, it's actually listed as 'I've Only Just Began', but never mind. The label itself has undergone a further transformation, having now lost the fluffy clouds and sunshine that graced 'Take It Cool' in favour of plain black and white lettering. The B side (or 'Bottom Side' as it's still referred to) is called 'I Can't Afford to Quit', and the writing on both is credited just to D. Pinnock.

The production credit reads 'Arranged and Produced by Tyrone for Harlesden Sound Production', which may well be the first reference to the 'Harlesden Sound' that Tyrone was apparently keen to promote as a local rival to the likes of Motown and Philly. The Top Side is described as a 'Limited Edition Monster Mix, 1980's style', while the Bottom Side is a 'Limited Edition Roots Mix, 1980's style', both of which descriptions are equally meaningless.

At the bottom of the label are the legends 'Marketed by Island Manufacturing' and 'Distributed by Spartan Records'. When I first saw the word 'Island' I jumped rather excitedly to the conclusion that somehow Tyrone had struck a deal with Chris Blackwell's mighty Island organisation, the home of Bob Marley and countless other top-flight reggae stars. But a little thought convinced me otherwise, because if that was the case it was a bit odd to refer to them as 'Island Manufacturing' and even if it was Island Records, surely they would have taken responsibility for distribution as well? I decided that the chances were that 'Island

Manufacturing' were probably some kind of light engineering company that just happened to be based down the road in Harlesden. Spartan Records were much easier to track down: they were a company set up in mid-1978 by a guy called David Thomas specifically to distribute records from the vast army of independent labels that had sprung up in the wake of the punk explosion. Clearly, Tyrone was beginning to think big.

I thought it might be interesting to visit the site of the Gangsterville Music Arcade to see what it looked like these days, so I hopped on a train to Kensal Green. Number 994 turned out to be a bar – to be more precise, a Portuguese Bar, situated right next door to the Benfica Restaurant and Tapas Bar. It seems that, in one of those small-scale mass migrations that makes London so continually fascinating, the African Caribbeans have moved out and the Portuguese – along with their co-linguists, the Brazilians – have moved in. Just down the road from where Gangsterville used to be, there is now the 'Delicies de Portugal' delicatessen, the Galpão Brazilian bar and kitchen, and the Manos Grill, featuring Portugese chicken, piri-piri style. Further back towards Kensal Green tube station, there was also the Sunrise hair and beauty salon, offering a Brazilian blow dry. I'll let you make your own jokes about that one.

And no-one in the bar had heard of Gangsterville at all. All evidence of Tyrone and the Harlesden Sound had vanished into thin air.

'I've Only Just Begun/Began' starts off in the usual way, with a percussion flourish giving way to a backing track. However, there's a significant difference this time around. Ladies and gentlemen: we have horns! The close-harmony chorus of 'Take It Cool' has given way to brass. To be honest, I'm not one hundred per cent sure it works, because wherever there are perky

The turning point was Bob Marley's 1977 album 'Exodus', which I bought mainly because of one track: 'Jammin''. 'Jammin'' almost immediately became one of my all-time favourites, and has stayed that way for the whole of the intervening thirty years. So what's so special about it? Superficially, it's an amazingly simple song. Over a lilting, chromatically descending bassline in a minor key, Marley sings a straightforward, almost banal, lyric, the message of which can be summed up as saying that his band are all jammin', jammin' in the name of the Lord, and that he hopes that we like jammin' too. In other words, they're all having a good time, the Lord has said it's OK to have a good time, so why don't we all join in and have a good time ourselves?

What elevates this above all else is the extraordinary combination of tight and loose musicality going on at the exact same time. Sure, the overriding initial impression is that it's a pretty free-and-easy number, just thrown together a few minutes before the recording. However, when you listen more closely, you begin to appreciate the ferocious level of disciplined collective musicianship that The Wailers are bringing to the party. Every single drum fill is in just the right place - even if the right place isn't necessarily on the beat. The tempo switches between the different sections are completely seamless, and I would like to think that it was recorded in a single take.

'Jammin'' works because, quite apart from the fact that it's impossible to stay still whilst listening to that particular groove, it also stimulates your brain by sending out a highly complex emotional signal that pulls you in two directions at once. It's the kind of tension / resolution combination that you find in great classical music, or in top-flight jazz improvisation, except that with Marley and the Wailers, the tension and resolution are going on simultaneously and continuously. 'Jammin'' was, in the end, what made me start taking reggae music seriously, and I've been exploring it on and off ever since. In between bouts of prog, naturally; some things you just can't leave behind.

By the way, we did make it to Khartoum, where we observed the celebrated confluence of the Grey and the Brown Niles. Much to our surprise, we did succeed in meeting up with Martin in Luxor on the way back; these days he sits on all sorts of influential committees and sports a CBE, which is three letters more than either Tim or I have managed. What's worse, we both failed miserably in our attempts to get off with either of those Aussie chicks.

A Passage to Jamaica

According to John Stuart-Russell's account (remember him – the one who was last heard of fleeing from the Japanese invasion of Eastern Papua?), Philip Pinnock's ancestors were an 'ancient and distinguished family', who were granted the 'magnificently rich pasture lands of the dismantled Malvern monasteries' by Henry VIII. These quotes apparently come from a book with the unhelpful title of 'Queensland', with no author or date or any other information apart from the fact that it was found in the Oxley Library in Brisbane. And in case you're wondering what this story has to do with Australia, well, that's where some of the white Jamaican Pinnocks ended up. It also turns out that one of them, Charlotte, married a Henry Stuart-Russell, which at least explains what John Stuart-Russell was doing investigating the Pinnocks as well as providing a hint as to how he might have ended up in Eastern Papua.

But let's now go back to Malvern for a moment. I should perhaps warn you that there's a bit of History coming up, but I'll try to keep it reasonably brief. Don't worry: my only qualification in that subject is a Grade 6 'O' level, so I'm not about to get too over-ambitious.

It seems that the dissolution of the monasteries hit Malvern in 1539. In Volume 4 of a 1924 book entitled 'A History of the County of Worcester', it states that two years later, Henry VIII leased the site of the Priory of Malvern along with the grange of Nether Court to one Richard Berde for 21 years. However, only five years later, in 1544, Berde transferred his lease to William Pinnock, 'to whom the King granted the lands in fee in the same year'. Which was nice of him. According to the same book, Pinnock sold the lands the very next year to John Knottesford, and this is corroborated by an 1822 book by Mary Southall with the eccentrically punctuated title *of A DESCRIPTION of MALVERN, AND IT'S CONCOMITANTS; INCLUDING A GUIDE TO THE DRIVES, RIDES, WALKS AND EXCURSIONS; WITH A MAP OF THE WALKS; A PANORAMIC SKETCH OF OBJECTS FROM THE WORCESTERSHIRE BEACON, and other Embellishments*. I do hope you noticed that nice early example of the greengrocer's apostrophe, there, by the way. Falling standards, eh?

I was rather intrigued by the speed of the sale of the lands. Had Pinnock maybe got a few debts to pay? If he did, he clearly didn't leave himself enough working capital, because in 1546, only a year after the transaction, his name turns up twice in a list of debtors to the King:

Ric. Breame and Wm. Pinnock, 53s 4d. *Henwood, Warw.*

Wm Pinnocke, 4s. *St Sepulchre's, Warwick.*

In present day terms, based on a comparison of average earnings, that comes to a total of around £15000, which is pretty substantial – especially when one considers that this was some time before the days of easy wonga. It's worth making a mental note of it now, because later on we may find ourselves wondering if it's a portent of much worse things to come.

There's very little more information about William Pinnock, apart from a burial notice dating from 1578, which is round about the right date, although – unless I'm reading it wrong – it seems to place the burial in Steventon, which is in either Oxfordshire or Hampshire, some way from Malvern. I guess it could possibly be referring to the area of Ludlow called Steventon, although there's no guarantee that it existed in those days. More likely it refers to someone else altogether, because later research threw up a reference to a different William Pinnock, who was born in another Steventon altogether, in Berkshire.

According to the account in 'Queensland', James Pinnock, born in Reading in 1620, was a direct descendant of this William, and he was the one who upped sticks and set sail with his family for Bermuda in 1658. There's no hint as to why he took this bold step, although it's interesting to note that, again according to 'Queensland', a Pinnock from William and James' branch of the family was Speaker of the House of Commons at some point under Cromwell. It's just possible that on Cromwell's death in 1658, James stuck his finger in the air to check which way the wind was blowing and decided it was no longer wafting in the right direction. Alternatively, it's interesting to note that in John Stuart-Russell's genealogy, he also married Anne Powell in the same year, offering the prospect of a far more romantic explanation. Perhaps old man Powell didn't approve of the union and they ran off together?

Further evidence for at least a variation on this theory turns up in a book with the zippy title of *Monumental Inscriptions of The British West Indies*. This book, which – exactly as the title suggests – contains transcriptions of inscriptions on West Indian tombstones 'chiefly collected on the spot by Captain J.H.Lawrence-Archer' and was published in 1875, at which point one assumes it must have roared to the top of the bestseller lists. Page 239 (of 470) reproduces a family tree located on a tombstone in St Andrew's Church at Halfway Tree, Jamaica, which states that James married Anne in *Barbados* in 1658.

Even more interesting, there are some unsubstantiated assertions in various online sites to the effect that Anne Powell was actually born in Barbados. By an odd coincidence, the first English ship to touch the island – in 1625 – was commanded by Captain John Powell. Not only that but the first ship to actually land, two years later, was commanded by his brother Captain Henry Powell, who brought with him eighty settlers and ten slaves, establishing the world's third ever parliamentary democracy in 1639. Possibly one of the smallest, too, I imagine. So it's not beyond the bounds of possibility that one of them had a daughter called Anne who caught the eye of James as he was passing through.

Whatever the truth of how they met, James and Anne didn't stay in Barbados long and soon proceeded to Jamaica, where they settled and raised a family. James Junior was born in 1660 and seems subsequently to have had the misfortune to bury three wives. His first two sons, one by each of his first two spouses, were both called James – I'm guessing that the first also pre-deceased the second. Neither of them had any issue, although the second one seems to have made it back to England to study at Oxford, matriculating at Pembroke College in 1730, according to university records. The last two sons, however, did survive long enough to start their own branches of the family. The first of these was Thomas, born to Mary in 1714, and the second one, born to Elizabeth in 1720, was Dog-Face Phil.

This is Lovers Rock

Not content with running the Gangsterland Musical Arcade and the Venture label, to say nothing of producing most of the records on that label – much like, I guess, Manfred Eicher of ECM – Tyrone also fancied himself as a singer. He cut a few solo discs, but those are of little interest to us right now because the object under study is not one of them. No, it is the only work by the vocal group Eargasm.

Savour that name, ladies and gentlemen. If there was ever a group name that screamed 'Lovers Rock', it would have to be Eargasm. It's a name that's been used countless times since and it would have been really cool to claim that this, in 1980, was the very first recorded usage of the word. However, I have since tracked down an earlier one – the title of Johnnie Taylor's 1976 album, featuring his certified platinum smash hit 'Disco Lady' as the opening track – which is a bit of a shame, as it would have been quite something to have Dennis potentially cited as an original source in the OED. However, I think we can still applaud our lot for being early adopters of the word.

Eargasm was a trio, consisting of Dennis Pinnock, Tyrone and another chap simply going by the name of Snoopy. Information on Snoopy was hard to come by as he was another of these people who are essentially a needle in Google's haystack. There were, frankly, an awful lot of Snoopy references out there and after a considerable amount of searching, I had to admit defeat, having found out absolutely nothing about him, apart from a brief biography on the SongCast website which described him as a Basildon Essex boy and former Black Echo music journalist as well as a very good singer, DJ and songwriter. The Eargasm record was apparently his debut single.

I have to say I was mildly disappointed when I received my eBay copy of the Eargasm record, because it came in a boring brown cardboard sleeve decorated with Venture Records' fluffy-white-cloud-and-sunshine-logo. This was in marked contrast to the back and white picture sleeve image on Tapir's online reggae discography showing the Eargasmic trio posing moodily amid the branches of a tree. Intriguingly, one of the three – the one squatting on the ground at the base of the tree – appeared to be white – or at least mixed race. If I had come across this record early on in my quest, it might well have caused me to jump to some entirely incorrect conclusions. However, by the time I obtained it, I'd already got hold of evidence from a couple of other picture sleeves – of which more later – that almost certainly identified one of the black guys in the tree as our Dennis. However, which of the remaining two was Tyrone and which was Snoopy remained, for the moment, a complete mystery.

The title of Eargasm's only single is 'This Is Lovers Rock', and it's a 12" disc on Venture Records, catalogue number EAR 26, and it came out in 1980. No songwriters are credited, although the record is 'Produced & Arranged by D. Tyrone for Harlesden Sound Production' and it's a 'Limited Edition Eternity Mix / Deadly Medley No. 1 / 1980's style'. Once again, it's marketed by Island Manufacturing and distributed by Spartan records. The two sides of the record have for this release reverted to conventional nomenclature, A and B, and the B side is called 'Name That Tune', supposedly performed by the wonderfully-named 'P Pop & The Beagle'. Credits are identical to the A side, except that this is 'Deadly Medley No. 2'.

Oh hang on a moment. According to the cardboard sleeve,

the record is 'MARKETED AND MANUFACTURED BY ISLAND RECORDS MANUFACTURING', so my original assumption was completely wrong: Island Records were involved after all. Exactly why they didn't distribute it as well is, however, a complete mystery, because one can't help feeling that things might have turned out a bit differently if that had happened, because Island were most definitely the Big Boys in the reggae playground at the time.

The first thing that has to be said about 'This Is Lovers Rock' is that it is EPIC: there are all of ten minutes twenty-eight seconds of it. Fortunately, it's all rather lovely. The production is very reminiscent of Gamble and Huff's classic Philly sound, and there's more than a hint of The Stylistics about the vocal harmonies. It's a very sophisticated package altogether, and it's hardly surprising that according to the NME website, it was a favourite party hit back in the day, just behind Janet Kay's 'Silly Games' and Sugar Minott's 'Good Thing Going'. But it still never quite made the crossover into the mainstream.

The record starts off with backing from some floaty echoed guitars that wouldn't sound out of place on a Steve Hillage record along with some judiciously placed 'pom' sounds from a syn-drum, overlaid with some harmony humming from our trio. Then the verse starts:

All these years we've been good friends
Moved together in the same neighbourhood
All at once, I can't believe my eyes
So much to realise.

Ah, she was right under your nose! Then later:

It's you, it's you I love
It's you, it's you I love
It's you, it's you I love
It's you, it's you I love

Eventually, we get the main chorus, which – for reasons which won't become clear until later – appears to have very little to do with any of the preceding theme:

Lovers rock
This is lovers rock
This is lovers, lovers lovers lovers rock

Truth to tell, the lyrics – for the most part anyway – aren't the most profound ones around, although later on, there's some odd vaguely biblical stuff about the river Jordan and having to go back home to Africa. After this, at around the 5:30 mark, there's an extended (and unattributed) direct quote from Matumbi's excellent 'Point Of View', including that gorgeous Glenn Miller-esque 'boo ba boo ba' background chorus.

The lead vocals swap around from one singer to the next and they all acquit themselves pretty well. According to the information given on the SongCast website, Tyrone takes the first lead, followed by Dennis Pinnock, with Snoopy bringing up the rear. But the real USP of Eargasm is the close harmony work, which is every bit as slick and sophisticated as the sweet soul produced on the opposite side of the Atlantic.

'Name That Tune' is, inevitably, a version of 'This Is Lovers Rock', and 'P Pop and the Beagle' are clearly Eargasm again, with the same backing track, although the lyrics sound as if they're being improvised, because frankly they descend into gibberish at times and it's actually a bit tiresome because there's not much in the way of dub fun and games. It is at least shorter than the A side, clocking in at a mere five minutes fifty-four.

What I didn't realise until much later was that 'This Is Lovers Rock' is actually a medley of songs that were around at the time of recording, set to a standard backing track. So no wonder they didn't make any kind of coherent sense. In a way, then, you could say that 'This Is Lovers Rock' was a much, much cooler precursor to the Dutch monstrosity known as 'Stars on 45' that was to hit the mainstream pop charts the very next year.*

Later on I found that there's also a 7" version of 'This Is Lovers Rock' (catalogue number EAR 726), with a somewhat more concise – and hence radio-friendly – version of the medley, which clocks in at a mere 3 minutes 37 seconds. This jumps straight (and pretty seamlessly) from the middle of 'Sweet Feelings' to the beginning of 'Mr Brown.' 'Name That Tune' survives largely unscathed, with only twenty seconds lost, although for the life me I couldn't work out where, or indeed why.

I also decided that for completeness' sake, I needed to get hold of a copy of the picture sleeve version of the 12". This version is on the Music Scene label, which we'll encounter in another context shortly, although it retains the same EAR 26 catalogue number as the original Venture edition. However, there are two important reasons why this later reissue is vastly superior. First of all, on the label, the B side has now become THE ROCKING SIDE, whilst the A side – in a stroke of absolute, complete and utter genius – has become THE BONKING SIDE. It's one of the great tragedies of our time that the shift to first CD and then MP3 has robbed us of the opportunity to have more music labelled in this way.

The second reason why this edition is better is that, along with the complete lyrics of both BONKING and ROCKING sides (including the sub Joycean gibberish that constitutes 'Name That Tune'), it has SLEEVE NOTES. And what sleeve notes they are too:

* 'Stars on 45', incidentally, is one of the few Wikipedia articles I've ever been tempted to contribute to. I added the bit about The Portsmouth Sinfonia's 'Classical Muddly', in case you're interested. These things are important.

This musical exercise was created for all you would be lovers on the dance floor, who often find it a near impossibility to pluck up the courage and ask the girl you've been watching and admiring all night for a dance. Suddenly a nice record is playing and with the Adrenalin flowing you approach the girl of your dreams, you ask her for a dance, to your surprise she says yes. While dancing you ask her name but by the time you gain her confidence to forward your intentions the record finishes. The D.J. puts on a record that completely destroys the mood, you stand there, what do you do now? You want to keep her with you, she smiles and starts to walk away probably out of your life for ever. Everything seems to be going wrong, how can you recapture the mood.

The solution – **THIS IS LOVERS ROCK!!!**

A specially created musical stimulant incorporating a well chosen selection of some great love songs, sensuously innovating with its infectious smooth and seductive melodic rhythmic overtones guaranteed to give you the time and inspiration even if you are a man of few words. By the time this record is finished you should know all there is to know:

His / Her Name / Phone No / Address / Age / Occupation / Hobbies
Vital Statistics / Likes and Dislikes / Weak Spots and Even her Bank Balance, etc.......

This record is dedicated to all the people who would like to have a good orgasmic experience.

If you know of any better sleeve notes than that, please do get in touch.

And that's it for Eargasm. The A side is as close to a classic as the Harlesden Sound came, I think, and it was a massive hit within the reggae community. Indeed, in *Black Music* magazine's charts for March 1980, it's straight in at number one in the Reggae 12" Singles charts, just ahead of 'Lovers Rock' by Sugar Minott, who clearly knew a good bandwagon to jump on when he saw one. But Eargasm still never quite made the breakthrough into the mainstream. Not long after this, Venture Records ceased production, although Dennis Pinnock and Tyrone were to make one final disc together. But that's another story.

The Secret World of a Generation

The excitement of finding Dennis Pinnock's possible address was followed by the inevitable air of despondency as it became abundantly clear that he either was no longer there or had no intention of responding to my overtures. It was entirely possible that he had moved on, leaving no forwarding address, but I was beginning to have a sinking feeling that he had taken one look at my letter and run a metaphorical mile from its contents. After all, from his point of view, this did look like a bit of a curious project.

So I cast around for other people who might be able to help. The first one I thought of was the veteran DJ David Rodigan, who I remembered from his 'Roots Rockers' show when I used to listen to Capital Radio back in the late 70s and early 80s. Coincidentally, this was the period when Dennis was in his heyday, so I thought it was worth a shot. His website had an e-mail address, so I wrote to him:

Hi,

I hope you don't mind me getting in touch, but I'm trying to find out some information about Dennis Pinnock for a book I'm writing. As you might guess, my interest was originally piqued by our shared surname, but my research has ended up going off into all sorts of other areas.

However, it's Dennis himself that I'm interested in right now. Are you familiar with his work? He was recording in the late 70s through to the 80s, and worked mainly with Tyrone and Tex Johnson. I'm also interested in what happened to them, and any of the others in the Harlesden Lovers Rock scene. I think I've gathered together all his recordings but I'd like to get some

kind of way of putting them all into context. I'd really appreciate any
pointers you could give me - would you be prepared to be interviewed?

Based on my experience to date, I wasn't massively hopeful of any response, but a week later he did in fact get back to me. Whilst it was massively cool to get a personalised reply from someone of Rodigan's stature, it wasn't entirely helpful. Although he did remember the name, he didn't have much knowledge of his work apart from a few tracks in the 70s. He concluded by saying that I probably had more information on Dennis than he did. So I really was on my own here. Still, e-mail from Rodigan, eh?

While I was agonising about what to do next, I decided to put my feet up and watch a movie. I'd come across it during one of my searches and I wondered if it might throw up any new clues as to what had happened to Dennis. The film was called 'The Story of Lover's Rock', with the enticing strapline 'THE SECRET WORLD OF A GENERATION AND THE BIRTH OF A REGGAE GENRE'. It was directed by Menelik Shabazz and it came out in 2011, although I couldn't remember any mention of it in the press; I must have missed the Guardian quote that adorns the cover: 'Menelik Shabazz has lovingly excavated the somewhat forgotten 70s subgenre of lover's rock'. Further research identified this as coming from a slightly lukewarm three-star review, but I think it deserved a bit more than that.

The film is a decent enough music documentary, even if the comic skits that punctuate it at regular intervals get a trifle wearing. But for anyone interested in that particular subgenre, it's an absolute goldmine of information. Almost all of the people interviewed are engaging and unusually articulate by music industry standards, especially Dennis Bovell, who really should have his own prime time music show. Forget Jules Holland – give the gig to Mr Bovell. Unfortunately there's very little archive material and most of the concert footage comes from the present day – which does at least go to show that Janet Kay has most definitely still got it.

Sadly there's no mention whatsoever of Dennis Pinnock – I hadn't really expected there to be – but just after the eight minute mark, someone connected with him does appear. It's none other than Snoopy out of Eargasm, although interestingly he's billed purely as a journalist with *Black Echoes* magazine. He is, however, quite unmistakeably a grown-up version of the white guy squatting on the ground beneath the tree on the cover of 'This Is Lovers Rock'.

Not only that, but at just after twenty minutes in, Paul Dawkins out of Four in a Row pops up on stage singing. So even if there's no sighting of Pinnock, that's two of his collaborators on screen. This gave me an idea. What if Menelik Shabazz was on Facebook? Granted, my previous forays there hadn't been massively successful, but perhaps this time around I might have a bit more success. Also, I potentially had some assistance this time, because it turned out that we had one Facebook friend in common, another writer who'd friended me a while back, presumably on the basis that we in turn had a significant number of writer friends in common.

So I messaged Menelik Shabazz. By now, I was feeling a bit more confident about showing my hand about the project, so this is what I said:

Hi,

Hope you don't mind me getting in touch, but I've just been watching your Lovers Rock film for research purposes and I've thoroughly enjoyed it - one of the best music docs I've ever seen in fact. [Creep – JP]

The reason I was watching it was that I'm writing a book which was inspired by my discovery years ago of Dennis Pinnock, the Lovers Rock singer. I was intrigued as to how my name crossed the race boundary and I also wanted to see if I could track him down.

I've pretty much sewn up the name thing - inevitably it centres around slave owners in Jamaica (unrelated to me as far as I can tell, which is something I guess) - but I still haven't quite managed to make contact with Dennis.

I did notice a couple of people on the film who worked with him, however - Snoopy and Paul Dawkins - and I'm wondering if you could put me in touch with either of them? Also, would you be prepared to be interviewed for the book yourself? Did you come across a guy called Tyrone in your researches?

Whilst I was awaiting his response, I had a peek at his friend list and – joy of joys – I noticed that there was a certain Paul 'Snoopy' Nagle there. However, I can't say I was massively surprised to find out that he was unmessageable. That would have been way too easy. I guess I could have tried friending him, but without any explanation for doing so it would have just looked a bit odd. However, he did also turn out to be on – oh dear – Myspace. So I sent him a message there:

Hi,

Apologies for bothering you, but...

I saw you being interviewed in that excellent Lovers Rock film the other day and I realised that it was indeed you that was in the group Eargasm along with my namesake Dennis Pinnock. I've been trying to track Dennis down for some time now, basically because I've been intrigued by the way the surname crossed the race boundary and I've ended up writing a book about it (I've had other stuff published already, BTW.)

Anyway, part of the book is a quest to find Dennis P, and I'm wondering if you still have any contact with him. I've tried sending a letter to his last known address, but I haven't heard anything back yet.

Also, would you be interested in being interviewed for the book yourself?

Cheers,

Jonathan Pinnock

PS Would have messaged you on Facebook, but your account is locked down against that kind of thing :)

Two weeks on, however, the message remained resolutely unread, alongside my equally ignored missives to G Vibes and Winston 'Saxton' Rose. It also seemed that Menelik Shabazz wasn't playing ball either. Where on earth could I turn to next?

Whitesmiths and Whimseymen

It took just over a month for the Church of Jesus Christ of Latter -Day Saints to locate my microfilm and get it shipped over to the UK. In the meantime, the General Register Office had sent me my copy of the marriage certificate for John Pinnock in 1840. Sadly, this turned out to be to someone called Mary Jones, which wasn't promising. Indeed, his father turned out to be an Edward Pinnock, which almost certainly ruled him out altogether.

However, I did find out that another John Pinnock (or possibly the same one) had got married in Dudley in 1844, so I ponied up a further £9.25 for a copy of the certificate for that one. But once again, John and Harriet's marriage proved to be elusive, as this one was to a Mary Brown. Pausing only to wonder at the apparent obsession of John Pinnocks with women called Mary, I did note that both bride and groom were resident in Snow Hill, Dudley, which matched John Pinnock's address at the time of the 1841 census. Not only that, but John's father was also called John, which fitted nicely as well.

John's profession was given as 'whitesmith', which was another new one to me. According to the list of old occupations that I'd used previously, this was the same as a tinsmith, which didn't quite seem to fit. Not only that, but there was nothing on the W page that came close to rivalling N for comedic value, although I did like the term 'whimseyman' for the man who drove the winding gear that carried men and materials up and down mineshafts. In fact, Wikipedia was more help this time, explaining that the term 'whitesmith' also referred to someone who did finishing work on iron and other 'black' metals, which seemed to slot very well into the general theme of iron-based work in Dudley.

But it still seemed a bit unlikely that this John Pinnock would turn out to be the one that subsequently married Harriet, as his first child was born in 1846. Then again, what if that child turned out to be Mary's rather than Harriet's? Given mortality rates on those days, it seemed entirely possible and indeed further research showed that a Mary Brown did die in Dudley in 1848.

So I searched a bit wider for marriages involving men called John Pinnock in Dudley, and finally in 1858, I found another one that matched. Not only that, but on the same page of the registry, there were only two possible choices for a partner and one of them was called Harriet Goold. The gap between Mary's death and the marriage to Harriet also cleared up the mystery of where John's wife was at the time of the 1851 census; the simple answer was that he didn't have one. In addition to this, the age of John's son Thomas at the time of that census – two – hinted that his mother Mary might well have died in childbirth. In fact, at the time of the 1851 census, it seems that Harriet Goold was working as a servant in the household of one William Millward, also aged 32, and his six-year-old daughter Hannah.

The fact that my step-great-great-grandmother once worked as a servant was strangely comforting. I know that entering service involved at least some degree of personal choice, and that the life generally didn't involve being shackled in some foreign field, but it was at least part of the same continuum as being a slave. These people couldn't really be connected to James and Philip, surely?

The downside was that this meant that in order to establish once and for all that I had the right parents for John Pinnock, I would have to purchase a copy of yet another marriage certificate, that of John and Harriet. This was getting to be an expensive business, but at least I was pretty sure I had the right one this time.

Just over three weeks later, the certificate arrived. The good news was that it almost certainly was the right one, because this John Pinnock gave his rank or profession as 'Agent', which matched the mysterious job description given in the 1861 census. Not only that, but he was described as a widower. Perfect! The bad news, however, was that both parents' names were simply given as 'Deceased', which was not remotely helpful.

However, by this point, the microfilm had arrived, so it was time to prepare for my voyage into the heart of darkness that is Stevenage.

Getting a Feeling

Dennis Pinnock's final record with Tyrone was on the Ambassador label, catalogue number EMB 7778, and according to Tapir's discography came out in 1980, the same year as the last of their joint ventures on, well, Venture. Don't get too excited about that catalogue number, by the way, because again according to Tapir, the numbers actually started at 7777. The label design, incidentally, has the word 'Ambassador' across the top in a font that would be entirely appropriate for a low-rent Streatham nightclub. The writing is credited to D. Pinnock, and the performance to Dennis Pinnock with 'Musical Backing by Elements'. It is also 'Prod. & Arr. By TYRONE for Harlesden Sound Productions', as well as being '1980s Style' and a 'LIMITED EDITION'. The B side has similar credits and is called 'Saturday Night Feeling'.

The really exciting thing on the label, however, is the legend 'Taken from Forthcoming LP "Dennis The Menace"'.

However, no such LP has ever turned up in my searches so I guess we can assume that it never happened. Whatever the reasons, it's clear that Tyrone was developing some serious ambition on the back of the success of Eargasm, as he took out a quarter-page advert in July's *Black Music* magazine to advertise his forthcoming attractions. His own 'I Need a Woman Tonight' ('HARDEST TUNE IN HARLESDEN') tops the list, followed by Dennis' 'The Feeling' ('HAVE YOU GOT THE FEELING?') and finishing with the enigmatically titled 'Say Love/Say Love/Crappy Song' by Elements (who would seem to be Tyrone's new house band following the departure of Tradition for hopes of glory at RCA). The advert concludes with the declaration that 'It's Gonna Be A Long Hot Summer'.

The music itself is well up to the standard we're coming to expect, however. After a brief drum intro, it settles into a relaxed, minor-key groove with some nice piano triplet grace notes on top, courtesy of – one assumes – Elements. The usual wordless vocalising comes in over this and then the close-harmony chorus starts:

I've got – I've got the feeling,
I've got – I've got the feeling,
The feeling to love you,
Oh yeah, the feeling to believe in you

But hang on, what's this?

Don't say, don't say you're going,
Don't say, don't say you're leaving
Because I need you
Oh yeah, I really need you

Well, I guess that explains the minor key. There isn't a lot more to the lyrics in fact, apart from some stuff about his love being reserved for her followed by a repeat of everything else. In fact, it's pretty much an instrumental track for the second half of the disc until Dennis chips in with a half-hearted rap over the fade right at the end. It's a nice song with quite a wistful vibe to it.

'Saturday Night Feeling' is a much jollier affair, which is odd because as far as I can tell, it's exactly the same backing track. However, this time around, Dennis starts straight off with a bit of a toast:

Turn on the water!
And dig this musical scorcher!

Which, interestingly enough, is precisely the same acclamation that kicks off *P Pop and the Beagle*'s 'Name That Tune.' Still, he wastes no time before launching straight into the song proper:

Eh, eh, are you feeling?
Eh, eh, are you feeling all right?
Say are you feeling OK?

We see we're going down to the blues,
So put on your dancing shoes.
We see we're going down to the blues,
So put on your dancing shoes.

'Cos it's a Sat'day night feeling
'An it's a Sat'day night feeling.

There's every chance I've mis-transcribed that, too, because Dennis is adopting a much more conversational, idiomatic Jamaican style of delivery here. But it works well, and it's a testament to his skill and versatility as a singer that he can switch so easily between the two, even when the accompaniment doesn't change at all.

The song continues on for another couple of minutes, very much in a rapping, semi-improvised style. And then a female voice unexpectedly joins in with a counterpoint that goes something like this (again I may have not got the words entirely correct):

One pound of rice
One pound of rice
I need some dancing that be nice,
I need some dancing that be nice,
One pound of meat,
One pound of meat,
For he's a dancer that is sweet
See he's a dancer that is sweet

There's no clue on the record as to her identity, and indeed that's her sole contribution to the disc, following which she presumably collected her session fee and went off home. After about five minutes or so, Dennis leaves the work to Elements and they play out the remainder of the song as an instrumental as per side A, and that's it for 'Saturday Night Feeling'.

This is another really good collaboration between Pinnock and Tyrone, and it's a damn shame they didn't go on to make that LP together. Might have been quite something.

Curiously, 'The Feeling' turned up again eight years later, on the Music Scene label, catalogue number MKS 62549. The two sides of the disc are designated 'Smooching side / Side A' and 'Spying side / Side AA'. The 'spying side' isn't by Dennis at all; instead it's given over to a track by Elements called 'Keeping A Watch Over You', which presumably also dates back to 1980.

This time around, it's described as being 'Mixed by the Groosome Twosome', who we've encountered before, albeit spelt slightly differently, on 'Pinnock's Paranormal Payback'. Mixing, however, is an unusual description for what actually happens here. Basically, about halfway through, at the point where in the original version it would have gone into that long instrumental run-out, there's a sudden crash of gears and it shifts into 'Saturday Night Feeling'. It's essentially the musical equivalent of those dodgy cut-and-shut second-hand cars that are actually made out of two damaged ones welded together. Still, at least it means that you get pretty much all of the content from both sides of the original disc on one, leaving room for the Elements track on the other. Then again, the Elements track is pretty unexceptional, so I'm not sure if it's actually worth it.

And that record concluded the entire output of the creative partnership of Pinnock and Tyrone. There were no clues as to what might have precipitated the break-up, or indeed what put the kibosh on that LP deal. But without talking to the man himself, it was unlikely that I'd ever find out.

Breakthrough!

Why, oh why was no-one talking to me? I was beginning to develop a bit of a complex about this whole project. Did I look a bit peculiar? Did I smell funny? Was I that odd, slightly whiffy bloke in the queue at the Post Office with a poorly-developed sense of his own personal space who insisted on telling me detailed anecdotes about his – admittedly unusual – career procuring girls for softcore pornography shoots (and yes, this really did happen to me on the very day I wrote this episode)?

However, there were still a few more angles from which to approach the problem. Maybe if I could get hold of Tex Johnson, he could help me out – especially since he'd worked with Pinnock more recently than the likes of Tyrone and Snoopy. The problem was that any search for Tex Johnson tended to come up with links to material about the legendary jet-age test pilot Alvin M. ('Tex') Johnson (1914 – 1998), famous for rolling a prototype Boeing 707.* Now I bow to no-one in my admiration of people like Chuck Yeager, but on this occasion I was looking for someone with the reggae right stuff and this wasn't helping. I tried narrowing the search by looking for 'Tex Johnson reggae', but this found nothing more than a load of links to his solo work, plus an intriguing feature on the Trojan website about Matumbi which revealed that he'd been a founder member, leaving some time before they found real fame.

The extensive list of credits on the covers of the two singles by Four In A Row suggested another way in. The name Ciyo

---

* Check it out on YouTube – it's pretty impressive.

seemed particularly unusual, and he turned out to be very straightforward to track down; indeed the first hit on Google for that one name was for the website of 'Ciyo Brown – Jazzy, Reggae, Soulful, Guitarist, Vocalist & Composer', which had to be him. Interestingly, there was a Facebook link on his website, so I went to take a look at his profile. He turned out to be messageable, so – once again – I contacted him:

This may sound a bit weird, but are you the same Ciyo who worked with Tex Johnson back in the 80s? I'm trying to find out more about my namesake Dennis Pinnock, of Four In A Row, and I noticed your name on the credits for their singles (and also your very distinctive guitar playing).

I'd really be interested in anything you could tell me about that time for a book I'm writing.

Then it struck me that Tex Johnson might be on his friend list, and – joy of joys – he was. So I messaged him as well:

Apologies for bothering you, but would I be right in thinking you're the same Tex Johnson who ran Discotex records back in the 80s? My reason for asking is that I'm trying to find out more about my namesake Dennis Pinnock, who recorded several records for you.

Are you still in touch with him? I'd be really interested in anything you could tell me.

Naturally, what I did next was have a quick skim through Tex Johnson's friend list. I probably don't need to tell you who I found there, right under my nose, after defying all previous Facebook search attempts. The picture was of an older man than I'd seen previously, but it was definitely still Dennis Pinnock, even including the trademark bling around his neck. So I sent him the same message that I'd previously conveyed by snail mail. I added this on the end, having forgotten to say so before:

I forgot to mention in the letter that I really like your work. I'm surprised

you never achieved a crossover into the mainstream. Anyway, I would be
really interested to meet you - would appreciate a reply either way.

Surely one of these three guys would get back to me? And just for good luck, I sent a friend request to Paul 'Snoopy' Nagle, although I wasn't too hopeful about that one as there was no way of explaining why I was trying to get in touch with him.

And then I had another inspiration. Now that I knew Snoopy's real name, I could Google him, and it turned out he had a LinkedIn account. Now I'm not a massive fan of LinkedIn – it's a bit like Facebook without pictures or conversations, and as Alice in Wonderland remarked, what good is a book without pictures or conversations? Still, I'm on there – mainly connected to people who wear suits to work instead of scruffy jeans, it's true – but I briefly wondered if I could hook up with Snoopy there as an alternative to Facebook.

However, it turned out that I didn't even need to do that, because there was a link to the website of his organisation there, and that website had a phone number on it. So I called the number and after a couple of rings, someone answered.

'Is that Paul Nagle?' I said.

Amazingly, it was. Not only that, but he readily agreed to be interviewed. At last I was making some real progress.

Too Many Goddamn Pinnocks

In the process of building up my collection of Dennis Pinnock records, it slowly became apparent that there was a potential complication that I would have to address at some stage. That complication had a name, and its name was Delroy.

You see, Dennis Pinnock was not by any means the only Pinnock with a recording career, and I'm not talking about Classical Trevor here, because he doesn't count (seriously, he doesn't – not in this context anyway*). No, I'm talking about Delroy Pinnock, who has an unfortunate habit of turning up on mislabelled eBay listings, causing me to get briefly excited about a new Dennis Pinnock disc before having my hopes cruelly dashed. Because Delroy also seems to have had a pretty extensive recording CV despite – like our mutual namesake – never having actually made it to a full-blown album.

Also like Dennis, his records seem to have acquired a bit of a cult status. For example, a copy of the ultra-rare orange vinyl 12" of 'Babylon Walls' seems to have sold for the astounding sum of £142 on eBay back in 2008. Curiously, this record is combined with a recording of Errol Bellot's 'Gimme'. Errol Bellot – or as I like to think of him, Errol 'Failed to reply to my Facebook

---

* In the interests of completeness, I should also mention Phoebe Pinnock, the lead singer of Aussie heavy metal band Heaven the Axe, and my own second-cousin-once-removed Owen Pinnock, half of 90s house outfit Grand Larceny. However, neither of these belong to the vast army of musical Pinnocks-of-Jamaican-origin, so I've stuck them in a footnote instead. Hope they don't mind.

message' Bellot – was one of the other stars on the Oxford Party bill back in 2002. So might he have worked with both Pinnocks? Or was that reference to Dennis in Oxford a misprint? Was it in fact Delroy who was there on that day? I guess that would at least explain the failure of any of them to get back to me.

I thought I really ought to get hold of a copy of one of Delroy's records, and I managed to find one a CD single of his from 2000, called 'Live in Peace'. The song is credited as being written by 'D. Pinnock, J. Pinnock and L. Pinnock'. One of the backing vocalists is Hugh Pinnock. Good grief. How many Pinnocks were there out there in the reggae business?

The CD is on the Clearsounds label, catalogue number CLR CDS1 – not a number that exactly screams 'major label'. Indeed, the CD sleeve is something of an abomination, consisting of an ancient map of Africa obscured by an orange swirl, superimposed on a fake parchment on which are written the lyrics of the song. The whole deal is topped by Delroy's name and tailed by the title of the CD, both of them rendered in a strange gloopy font complete with air bubbles. Well, I guess this must have seemed like a really neat idea at the time.

As for the music itself, I get the feeling that he would have loved to have been late period Bob Marley, the main problem being that he missed out on that particular opportunity. The other problem is that on the basis of this one CD, the music is, frankly, a bit bland. The CD comes with a couple of mixes, the only one of which that seriously adds any value being the '2001 Dancehall Mix feat. Headtop' where the aforementioned Headtop kicks a bit of life into things by overlaying a nicely-judged rap. Could have done with a bit more of Headtop, to be honest.

However, Delroy was only the start of it. I also tracked down a compilation CD with the enticing title 'Gully Slime', part of the

'Riddim Driven' series marketed by VP Records ('Miles ahead in reggae music'). Every track on this album is produced by Mark Pinnock. Indeed, M. Pinnock is listed as one of the writers on every single track too, so it's most definitely his baby.

Once again, the CD cover is not promising, given that the background is – as per the title of the CD – an image of some kind of greenish primordial slime, with the names of the artists involved overlaid in a barely legible futuristic font. The catalogue number, however, is VPCD2337-2, indicating a promising degree of longevity in the label. Indeed, the back cover contains images of several other CDs in the 'Riddem Driven' series.

'Gully Slime' is a very strange album indeed. It purports to be the work of no less than fourteen individual artists, from Tony Matterhorn and Elephant Man through to the fantastically-titled Captain Barkey & Wickerman, but EVERY SINGLE TRACK has the same chunka-chunka-chunka backing, courtesy of (one assumes) Mr Pinnock. This would certainly explain all those co-writer credits, but it doesn't exactly make for a varied listener experience. There's not much joy to be had in the lyrics either, as the rapping is for the most part pretty impenetrable apart from the occasional exclamation of the word 'BLOODCLAAART'. All in all, I have to say that it's not a massively attractive package.

More problematic still is the Canadian jazz singer Densil Pinnock, who actually changed his name to Denzal Sinclaire around the turn of the millennium. His music is pretty cool and sophisticated, in fact – very reminiscent of Nat King Cole. But I was intrigued as to why he'd changed his name in mid-career, because it seemed a bit of a risky move. I couldn't locate any statement giving his reasons, and indeed on his website the name Pinnock is airbrushed out of existence, along with any reference to the two albums he recorded under that name, 'I Waited for You' and 'Mona Lisa'.

So I e-mailed his management to see if they could shed any light on this:

Hi,

I wonder if you can help me. I'm writing a book, part of which covers the way in which the name Pinnock crossed the race boundary. I know that Mr Sinclaire used to be called Pinnock, and I'm wondering why he changed it. Was it because of the connection with slavery, or for some other reason? I'd be really fascinated to know.

Many thanks in advance.

While I was waiting for a reply, things took another bizarre turn: even Simon Cowell was getting in on the act. It turned out that 2011's UK X Factor winners, Little Mix, had a Pinnock in their ranks. According to ITV's official web page about the group, Leigh-Anne Pinnock cites Justin Bieber as her favourite artist/ musical inspiration, so perhaps we should not dwell on her for too long. Except to note that her offering of 'heel/toe dance moves' as a party trick is singularly less ambitious than her bandmate Perrie Edwards (presumably no relation to the late Percy), who does goat impressions. Sorry, Leigh-Anne. The goat wins every time.

And that wasn't the last of the singing Pinnocks, by any means. Much, much later I came across the work of Don-A V a.k.a. Donna V a.k.a. Donovan Pinnock. Don-A V released several singles in the late 90s and on into the new millennium, including the 2000 album 'Cry for Tomorrow' – on the Studio One label, no less – as well as a 'Greatest Hits' compilation which, oddly, features none of the songs on 'Cry for Tomorrow'. It also turned out that I'd hitherto overlooked the drummer with the acclaimed reggae band Beshara, Dixie Pinnock.

It didn't stop there, either, because I hadn't reckoned on the producer/engineer Laurel 'Peego' Pinnock, who seems to have been active from the late 80s through to the early 00s. Fans of really obscure artists might also be tempted by the oeuvre of Andrew Pinnock, whose entire output seems to consist of one record, 'I Will Give You Love', on the Indeka English label.

There's also the enigmatic producer N. Pinnock, whose name appears on the respective sole records by Earth Inheritance Band and Essence, both in 1980.

And then one of my writing chums alerted me to the existence of The Pinnocks, a gospel duo from Jamaica consisting of Pastor Fred and his wife Doreen. Their website is a treat and I do recommend that you check it out and maybe listen to a few sample tracks from their debut record 'The Holy Ghost'. According to the True Grace Promotions website, Pastor Fred and his wife won a singing contest at their local church in 2006, 'from there their talent begun to sore.' Well, if it's sore, best put some cream on it is what I say. I'm being unfair: their music isn't actually that bad and if weird hybrids of gospel and reggae are your scene, you will find much to admire here.

There were, it seemed, a lot of musical Pinnocks out there. Moreover, they were almost ALL apparently of Jamaican origin. And I haven't even started on the other high-achieving black Pinnocks. For example, at one point in the mid 2000s, the Jamaican athletics team could field a Pinnock at almost every distance. The actor Arnold Pinnock has appeared in several acclaimed films, including 50 Cent's vehicle 'Get Rich or Die Tryin'' and – ahem – the Christian fundamentalist epic 'Left Behind – World at War'. Hmmm. Let's just make that 'appeared in several films', then. Perhaps we'd be better off with Emil Pinnock, then, who co-starred with Danny Glover in 'Beloved'? Or, closer to home, there's always rising star of British television, Nicholas Pinnock.

In fact, setting aside Trevor's undoubtedly significant achievements in the world of classical music, the white branch of the family have made a pretty poor showing in general. And I haven't even mentioned the award-winning playwright Winsome Pinnock, have I?

Much to my surprise, Denzal Sinclaire eventually got back to me in person, with a long and thoughtful reply. For him, it wasn't anything to do with the slavery connection at all. It was more a case of having reached a certain point in his life where he wanted to take charge of his destiny and begin a new phase. From a practical point of view, I guess, changing your name from Pinnock to Sinclaire to signal a change of direction is a damn sight easier to manage than converting it from, say, Prince to that symbol thing, so I'd say he seems to have his head screwed on. And judging from the list of high-profile bookings listed on his very professional-looking website, he's doing rather well out of it.

In the end, though, out of loyalty to Dennis, and also owing to the more practical consideration that there were simply too many of the buggers, I decided not to pursue any of the others. I had to maintain some kind of focus to the project after all.

To the Victors, the Spoils...

After the break-up with Tyrone, Dennis seems to have gone quiet for a few years before deciding to give it another go. His comeback single is on Viking Records (catalogue number VIK 002), and unlike most of his output, it's a 7" disc. Information on Viking Records is hard to find, the problem being that there are thousands of other labels calling themselves Viking Records. To make matters worse, the usually reliable and exhaustively comprehensive Tapir's Reggae Discographies site makes no reference to Viking Records at all. In any case, given the number of Dennis' contribution, there's no guarantee that the catalogue for this particular Viking Records ever stretched to more than two releases. I also imagine that the use of a horned helmet as the logo for the label is far from unique in the world of Viking record labels.

The A side of the record is called 'Totally Disrespect', and it's credited to Dennis (Menice) Pinnock. I'm guessing that's just a misspelling, although it could be a subliminal assertion that he is, despite anything else you may have heard, a thoroughly nice chap. Engineering is by Fitzie, and it's arranged and produced by Victor Dee and Victor Viking (other significant Victors such as Hugo, Sylvester and Kiam being, one imagines, otherwise engaged). Presumably the label is named after the second of the two Victors.* The B side is simply called

---

* I'm also assuming, incidentally, that he is not the same Victor E. Viking who is the mascot of Northern Kentucky University. These Scandinavians get everywhere.

'Totally No Respect', and has no credit given to the singer. Incidentally, there are no writing credits on either side, so we may perhaps assume this is all Dennis' own work. Which is all fine, but is it any good?

The answer is that it's actually not bad at all. The song itself is a bouncy, inconsequential number which would probably get a bit annoying after a while, but Victor and Victor's production is competent and the backing is exemplary, even if there's just a little bit too much wood block in there for my liking. The lyrics are hard to make out, so I can't be one hundred percent clear as to the thematic content of the song, but given that it starts with 'Every day when you walk in town' and has a refrain of 'Total disrespect', I would imagine that it's something to do with the protagonist's girlfriend parading around the place in order to attract attention, to the detriment of their relationship. Something like that, anyway.

The B side is a genuine dub of the A side, rather than a replay of the backing track, although it doesn't exactly break new ground in terms of special effects. All in all, however, this is a very promising return to the recording studio for Dennis Pinnock. To the Victors, the spoils, then?

Well, no. For whatever reason, Dennis doesn't seem to have hung around with them for very long, because his next move was to hook up with another producer by the name of Tex Johnson, who ran the Discotex label. I'm guessing this name is derived from the combination of Disc and Tex and had absolutely nothing to do with 70s camp disco divas Disco-Tex and the Sex-O-Lettes, led by Sir Monti Rock III, who wowed the charts with 'Get Dancin'' and 'I Wanna Dance Wit' Choo (Doo Dat Dance)'. At least I fervently hope it doesn't.

Dennis' first disc for Discotex was a 12" called 'In & Out Of Love' (catalogue number DT18). Writing, arrangement and production credits go to Tex Johnson, and it's mixed by Lindel Lewis. It also features Ciyo and Keith Douglas on background vocals – remember those names, as we will encounter them again very soon. The first thing to note about this track is that it's very, very different from Dennis' work with Tyrone. There's a much lighter, jazzier feel to it. I'm not entirely sure if I prefer it, but the good thing is that Dennis is a sufficiently versatile singer to handle the shift in style with ease.

Basically it's a jaunty number about the dangers of falling in love too easily, resulting in a series of failed short-term relationships – although I'm slightly concerned that the backing vocalists seem to be singing that 'I think I've got the formula right'. The implications for society are not discussed, but I think we can draw our own conclusions. There's a lot of sparky interplay between Dennis's lead vocals and the backing provided by the guitarist (who is almost certainly Ciyo) and his backing vocalists. It has a certain charm, but it's not one of Dennis' stronger records. The B side claims to be a dub, but it's essentially the same as the A side, minus the lead vocals, credited to 'Discotex Band'.

The next logical step was to form another vocal group, and as we shall see soon, that's exactly what Tex and Dennis chose to do.

The Author, at St Pinnock, Cornwall

The young Jonathan Pinnock, oboist in the making

I HAVE just discovered that NME is pronounced "enema" in French. Does this explain a lot about French musical taste? — **BORIS O'PELICAN, Clare College, Cambridge.**

BETCHA won't print this letter upside down. — **DORIS THE PELICAN, Cambridge.** ■ *Dead right we won't mate. You call this a letter?* — M.B.

Letters to *NME*

Supertone Records, Brixton

Once home to the Gangsterville Music Arcade, Harlesden

Paul Nagle aka "Snoopy"

Tex Johnson, Mr Discotex

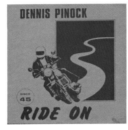

This musical exercise was created for all you would be lovers on the dance floor, who often find it a near impossibility to pluck up the courage and ask the girl you've been watching and admiring all night for a dance. Suddenly a nice record is playing and with the Adrenalin flowing you approach the girl of your dreams, you ask her for a dance, to your surprise she says yes. While dancing you ask her name but by the time you gain your confidence to forward your intentions the record finishes. The D.J. puts on a record that completely destroys the mood, you stand there, what do you do now? you want to keep her with you, she smiles and start to walk away probably out of your life for ever. Everything seems to be going wrong, how can you recapture the mood?

The solution – **THIS IS LOVERS ROCK!!!**

A specially created musical stimulant incorporating a well chosen selection of some great love songs, sensuously innovating with its infectious smooth and seductive sexual melodic rhythmic overtones guaranteed to give you the time and inspiration even if you are a man of few words. By the time this record is finished you should know all there is to know:-

> His / Her Name / Phone No / Address / Age / Occupation / Hobbies
> Vital Statistics / Likes and Dislikes / Weak Spots and
> even her Bank Balance, etc.......

This record is dedicated to all the people who would like to have a good orgasmic experience.

The original 'LOVERS ROCK' Disco 45 First of its kind by EARGASM
Vocals by Tyrone, Snoopy, D. Pinnock, (Eargasm)
Arranged and Produced by Tyrone
For Harlesden Sound Production, Copyright Control (MCPS) © ℗
Marketed by MUSIC SCENE
British Lovers Rock Music (BLRM)
T.K. Enterprises.

Lovers Rock, Sleeve Notes

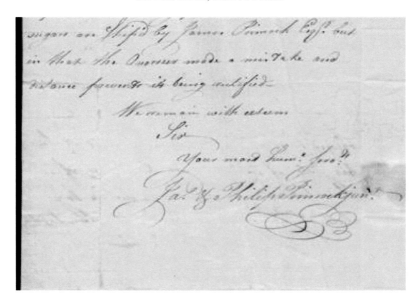

Letter to Samuel Munckley

The Pinnock Grave, Portishead Cemetery

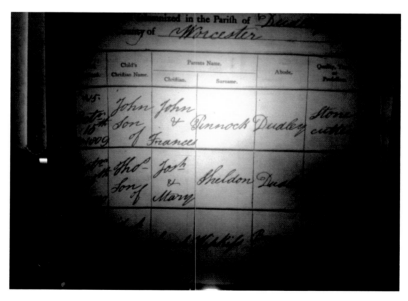

The Dudley line of the Pinnock family

This picture - possibly the most important in the entire book - was taken in the pre-selfie era by a friend of Dennis, following hopelessly inadequate instructions from the author as to how to use his camera.

Take it Cool

Swings and Roundabouts

Stevenage is the place where roundabouts go to die. A sterile urban wasteland covered by a patchwork of improbably-named trading estates, it's a place I have spent much of my life avoiding. However, when I used to live in St Albans, I was forced to go there on occasion, generally when the humungous 500-screen Cineworld complex was filling up space with a film that no-one else in Hertfordshire could be arsed to show.

As you approach Stevenage along the A1(M) you are greeted by the imposing and ever-so-slightly sinister Glaxo Smith Kline research centre. To get to the Church of Jesus Christ of Latter-Day Saints, you need to go past this on one side, and the Roaring Meg retail park (told you they had improbable names – apparently this one's named after a local stream, not, as I'd always thought, a cannon) on the other. The LDS place is unfortunately on the opposite side of the dual carriageway that you now find yourself on, so you have to go all the way down to the next roundabout, go through three hundred and sixty degrees and head back in the direction you came.

The Church is a bog standard modern ecclesiastical building on the side of a housing estate. The Family History Centre is tucked in at the back, with entrance through the car park. Despite the fact that it's only open two mornings a week, there was only one other car there. Still, at least that meant I wouldn't have to queue. I went in and found a dimly-lit room with four other occupants, two of whom, who were hard at work at a computer, turned out to be members of the church. The other two were a couple in their sixties who were intently studying a microfilm and bickering in the practised way that only couples who have been together thirty years and have now found themselves thrown together twenty-four hours a day and seven days a week as a result of retirement know how to bicker.

One of the two church people, an oldish chap with a slight paunch, stood up as I entered.

'Can I help you?'
'Yes, I ordered a microfilm.'
'Ah. What was the name?'
'Pinnock.'
'Ooh yes. A lot of Pinnocks in Hertfordshire. Had one over from the States recently to talk to the church, too.'
'What was his name?'
'Hmmm. Not sure. He was just Elder Pinnock.'

I quite liked that. In fact, I may take to calling myself Elder Pinnock from now on if I'm ever in need of a spot of extra *gravitas*.

Having located the microfilm, the assistant went to switch on microfilm reader number 3. However, this didn't seem to be working, so he proposed machine number 2 as an alternative. Unfortunately, number 2 was situated right next to the bickering couple, and the husband bridled at the threatened incursion into his territory, only just managing to hide his pleasure at the opportunity to bicker with another party. But after a considerable amount of faffing around with cables we managed to get number 3 hooked up to the power and I was shown how to use it.

It turned out to be quite straightforward to locate the birth records for Dudley, as they had been scanned in alphabetical parish order and then by date. However, there wasn't really any more useful information on the microfilm. In fact, the only new nugget was that my great-great-great-grandfather John was a stonecutter. All I can say is that that's one gene that's most definitely dropped by the wayside, because I can't imagine being able to do anything useful with my hands. I have fond memories of the time I tried putting together a flat-pack wardrobe and, pausing in mid-assembly to admire my work, watched as its profile gracefully mutated from rectangle to parallelogram to horizontal straight line.

Meanwhile, the couple to my left had just about avoided fisticuffs over the interpretation of the columns in a table on their microfilm and, with an exasperated cry of 'Oh, forget it!' from the wife, had simmered down again. I wound back my film and handed it back to the assistant and that was it for me and the Mormons. On the way back, I promised myself that I would console myself by watching a video of The Osmonds doing 'Crazy Horses' on YouTube. A friend of mine used to have a theory that if you turned the brightness on the television right down, you could get it so that only their teeth were showing. I've never actually tried this, though, because I so wanted it to be true and I was afraid it would turn out to be an urban myth.

As I drove away, I noticed the names of all the roads in the estate: Briardale, Buckthorn Avenue, and – good grief – Elder Way. Remarkably, it seemed that even the streets around these parts had been co-opted into the Church.

Back home, I went back to the Family Search website for one more try to find out some more about Stonecutter John Pinnock. Previously I'd tried to home in on him by linking him with Frances, but this time I simply searched for information on him with a wide range of birth dates – 1780 to 1795. And there he was, baptised on the 12th of March, 1786 in St Thomas' Church, the very same one that John Junior was baptised in, twenty-nine years later.

The parents of this John Pinnock were another Joseph and Mary combo (I'll resist the jokes this time), and in fact this was their second attempt at a John, the first one having only lasted from January 1783 to December 1785. So I dug a bit further and found a Joseph Pinnock who was buried in Dudley in 1813, aged 64. Chances are that he was also the same one that married Mary Ditheridge in St Thomas' Church in 1773. However, I couldn't find any reference to his birth in 1749, so the trail looked as if it was going cold again.

However, in another search for Joseph Pinnock born in Dudley, this time with no date restrictions, threw up some unexpected results. Because it seemed there were TWO MORE Joseph Pinnocks to take into consideration, both of whom were baptised in St Thomas' Church. The first of these was born to Joseph and Mary in 1776, three years into their marriage, making him John's big brother. The other one was born to John and Mary Pinnock in 1771. Wha – ? Who? I mean, WTF?

The only explanation had to be that John Pinnock was Joseph's elder brother, who had presumably taken the lead in marrying women called Mary. For a moment I wondered if perhaps John had died young, bequeathing his widow to his brother, but the discovery of the record of a marriage between John Pinnock and Mary Lavender in 1770 in St Thomas' Church disabused me of this notion. Still, I can't help feeling that family gatherings must have been more than a little confusing. In fact, the constant recycling of the same Christian names was beginning to make me feel that I'd accidentally stumbled into the middle of Gabriel Garcia Marquez's *One Hundred Years of Solitude*.

Anyway, this was actually pretty good news, because if I could find this John Pinnock's birth record, it would be as good as finding Joseph's. And amazingly, that's exactly what happened next. John Pinnock was born in 1745, four years before his presumed brother Joseph, to parents William and Hanah. But from this point it all gets a bit tricky. Assuming that William wouldn't have moved far from his birthplace, the only possibilities for his birth record seemed to be 1700 in Wick, near Pershore (parents – sigh – William and Sarah), 1718 in Wick, near Pershore (parents – sigh again – William and – double sigh – Mary) or 1723 in Kempsey (parents – even more sighing – John and Elisabeth). I guess it was even possible that the 1700 one from Wick was father of the 1718 one.

According to the AA route planner, Wick is 48 minutes down the M5 from Dudley, whereas Kempsey is a mere 37 minutes (also on the M5 – beware speed cameras). In either case it would still have been a bit of a trek by horse and cart. Even so, it wasn't beyond the bounds of possibility. The worrying aspect of this, however, was that we were getting dangerously close to the territory occupied by Dog-Face Phil's ancestors in Malvern – who were also, as it happened, quite keen on the name William. It was still by no means certain that we were unrelated.

Dog-Face Phil's Chequered Career

It's worth noting in passing that the account given by John Stuart
-Russell above in *A Passage to Jamaica* disagrees slightly with that
of F. J. du Quesnay, wherein James Pinnock Junior was born in
1691, not 1660. du Quesnay also spells Anne differently – as
Ann. I'm inclined to go with Stuart-Russell though, because that
would put James Senior fathering a child at 71 – not impossible, I
guess, but unlikely all the same. Indeed, as I trawled through all
these different accounts, it was becoming clear that some were a
lot less reliable than others, and that the phenomenon of Wiki-
vandalism might not be quite so new after all. It was perhaps only
a matter of time before a Pinnock was cited as the saxophonist
on Gerry Rafferty's 'Baker Street'.

There are even more sources to play with when researching
the career of Philip Pinnock himself, as he was – as I have
alluded to earlier – a Pretty Significant Bloke. We already know
from the *Daily Gleaner* that he was Speaker of the House of
Assembly at some point, but according to the 'Queensland' book,
he was also Chief Justice for a time as well. This is confirmed by
the *Magazine of Magazines* for July 1754, an excellent publication
which, as its name perhaps suggests, is a weird and wonderful
mishmash of articles including court reports, political
commentary, bad poetry and quack cures for both humans and
livestock, such as this mysterious 'Receipt for the GRAVEL' on
page 593:

TAKE of broom-feed; finely ground, as much in quantity as will lie upon the surface of a shilling, in a gill of the best white port, morning and evening.

This is followed by an account of the life of Pope SIXTUS V, incidentally.

The *Magazine of Magazines* is the sort of mad historical document that you could easily lose yourself in for several weeks, but we must sadly move on to page 664, where we find that Philip Pinnock was indeed appointed to the post of Chief Justice of Jamaica in that year, at the impressively early age of 34.

However, this does not seem to have been a propitious choice – at least if we believe what the Reverend George Wilson Bridges has to say about it in Volume Two of *The Annals of Jamaica*, dating from 1828. This book has, by the way, one of the best opening sentences of a historical work that I have ever read:

In the long career of vice and vigour, of error and oppression, I have at length reached the term of my labours, and have completed my design of bringing down the Annals of Jamaica, from the first blush of that morning which dawned upon the long night of transatlantic oblivion, to the present evening of its decayed and feeble existence.

Wow. I'm thinking his sermons must have been quite a hoot. More of that kind of thing and I might have tried a bit harder at that 'O' Level.

Anyway, it all kicks off on page 88, in the year of 1758, following the replacement of Lieutenant Governor Knowles (who presumably would have appointed Pinnock to his post) by

Lieutenant Governor Moore. Following his departure, Knowles was 'tumultuously burned in effigy' along with his ship, so one can assume that he was not a popular chap. According to Bridges' account, Moore seems to have subsequently taken a bucket and shovel to the Augean stables of Jamaican civic life, prompting this alarming statement:

> *The fountain of justice was once more cleansed by the removal of Pinnock, the corrupt chief justice, who was consigned to the ignominy which, in every age and country, has attended the character of an informer...*

Well, not quite. Philip Pinnock clearly lived to fight another day. du Quesnay's more sympathetic version of the story fails to mention Pinnock's tenure as Chief Justice at all, but says that prior to taking the office of Speaker, he was a member of the Council, 'in which office there seems to have been some unpleasantness while Roger Hope Elletson was Lieutenant Governor', which would have been in either 1766 or 1767. Oh dear. What now? Well, according to du Quesnay, it all came down to a disagreement over a money bill, in the course of which the Council passed a vote of censure on Elletson. The Lieutenant Governor responded in the time-honoured manner by suspending seven of them, including Pinnock.

du Quesnay goes on to say that Pinnock subsequently recovered from this new reverse and became Speaker twice, as well as representing St Ann and St Thomas-in-the-East and being Custos for St Andrew (as per the *Daily Gleaner* article). Clearly his rehabilitation was complete. Take that, Reverend Bridges.

Not only that, but whilst he was in office, he also managed to acquire a considerable fortune, if we are to believe the account given in *The Development of the British West Indies 1700 – 1763* written by Frank Wesley Pitman, PhD and published in 1917.

In a footnote to a description of the 'Gentlemens' Houses', the 'magnificent dwelling' of Philip Pinnock is singled out for special mention, noting that the cost to him was £25000. I fed this amount into a calculator I found lying around on the internet and based on equivalent earning power, such a mansion would apparently cost £40M in present day money, which would have made it one of the most expensive private dwellings on the planet at the time.

And yet, in 1777 he wanted to sell the house for £15000, desiring that 'his creditors might raffle for it'.

According to another account – on a website involved in the selling of properties on the Richmond Estate in St Ann – the writing had been on the wall for some time. In 1747, he'd bought this estate, later mortgaging it for the eye-watering sum of £120000 (just try to scale that one up – I have trouble believing it, to be honest) to the Hon. William Gray, the Provost-Marshal-General of Jamaica. Pinnock had been forced to sign that lot over to Gray in 1775 because he couldn't keep up with the payments. Karma was restored, however, in 1784 when Gray himself, who had subsequently divided the plantation into two estates, was forced to sell both to his major creditor when he also became financially over-extended.

I should perhaps add that it's by no means certain that the description given by Pitman refers to the St Ann estate, because according to an article in the *Daily Gleaner* of March 8th, 1983 ('From Sugar Estate to University'), he also seems to have purchased an estate in St Andrew in 1754. This seemed to have been an unwise investment because of deficiencies in the soil resulting in poor yields, and he sold it on not long afterwards. Before he did so, he changed the estate's name to 'Mona', although no-one is quite sure what the significance of this was. Either way, the name lives on to this day, as the main campus of the University of the West Indies.

Whatever the actual details of the various estates that he bought and sold, it's hardly surprising that when Pinnock died in 1778, he was a broken man. His life is summed up in Frank Cundall's 1904 *Biographical Annals of Jamaica*, thus:

> *PHILIP PINNOCK, speaker of the house of assembly from 1774 to 1778, and custos of St Andrew, was an example of the wealthy Jamaican planters who went from London from time to time and cut a dash on the proceeds of the cane-fields. He died almost a pauper.*

So much for 'The Dandy'. Not only that, but by the time he died, he had buried his wife, his son, one of his two daughters and one of his granddaughters as well. From the brief glimpses into his life that the various accounts give, I'm still not entirely sure what to make of him. He must have had a fair amount of charisma to hold on to so many public offices and to bounce back from more than one setback, but something smells a bit funny. You don't make and lose that kind of money by being nice to everyone.

And we've barely mentioned the vast pachyderm that's standing there in the room, wildly waving its trunk for attention. After all, Philip Pinnock's entire fortune was based on the labour of his slaves.

Four – In a Row

Following 'In & Out Of Love', the next step was clearly to put together a proper vocal group, and that presumably as how Four in a Row came into being. This was, as the name suggests, a foursome, with the line-up completed by Keith Douglas, Paul Dawkins and Tex Johnson himself. Information on Keith Douglas was hard to come by, but I'd spotted Paul Dawkins on Menelik Shabazz's documentary, so he was clearly still working. In fact, further research established that he was another refugee from Tyrone, having previously being a member of Tradition, as well as being lead singer with The Heptics. Tex Johnson was presumably the main man of the group, being the label boss.

The first of FIAR's (as I think we should call them, in order to add the requisite level of fanboy familiarity) records is a 12" called 'Love Is…' and it has catalogue number DT19. There isn't any explicit information as to when it came out, although judging from the presence of a DX7 synthesizer on it (and we'll see how I know this in a minute), it must have been at least 1983 (thank you, Wikipedia). Setting aside any speculation as to what might have happened during the wilderness years of the early eighties, let's take a look at the spiffy picture sleeve for clues.

The top of the front side of the sleeve (which is entirely in black and white) is given over to the words 'LOVE IS…' followed by a rather cool pastiche of one of those twee Kim 'Love Is…' cartoons. The bottom part gives the name of the groups and its members. But the middle is a picture of the lads themselves, posing casually – yes, in a row – wearing smart white matching polo shirts, each one leaning on the shoulder of the one to their left. Not all of them look at ease with this arrangement, it has to be said, although Paul Dawkins looks massively cool. Dennis Pinnock doesn't come out of it too badly either, with a distinct air of Sammy Davis Jr about him, including half a ton of bling around his neck.

Turning the cover over, we have another picture of the four of them. In a row. Again. This time, they're sitting down, in reverse order, with Dennis on the left hand end. Each one is holding out their right hand, and once again Pinnock and Dawkins seem entirely comfortable with the pose, whereas the other two would clearly rather be somewhere else altogether. Like now. Please. Anywhere. Frankly, both pictures are straight out of the Beginners' Guide to Boy Band Photography, but they're none the less charming for that.

Underneath the picture, however, it's clear that a muso has been at work, because the credits are about as long as those on Pixar's entire filmography strung together. Lead vocals are by Dennis Pinnock, Tex Johnson, Keith Douglas and Paul Dawkins. Background vocals, amazingly, are also by Dennis Pinnock, Tex Johnson, Keith Douglas and Paul Dawkins. Drum programming is by Ciyo and Lendel Lewis, bass by Spy, DX7 by Skully. Rythm (sic) and lead guitar by Ciyo and percussion by Ciyo. It's recorded, voiced and mixed at Mark Angelo's, where the recording and mixing engineer is Lindel Lewis.

(Deep breath.)

It's also arranged by Ciyo and produced by Tex Johnson in association with Ciyo for Discotex productions. The writing credits go to Dennis Pinnock, Keith Douglas, Melvin Brown and Tex Johnson, and it's published by Discotex Music. Marketing is by Discotex Records and distributed by Discotex Records, Jet Star, EMI, Marcus and Fat Shadow. ALL of the latter have their phone numbers supplied in case anyone fancies getting in touch with them, which is eminently practical. Finally (in small print) graphics are by Tony Nero (who I guess must be the same A. Nero who produced the cover for 'Ride On', and thus becomes the other missing link between Tyrone and Tex Johnson). Oh yes, and the photos are by Dan Harriot.

Yes, but what about the music? Well, it starts off with a unison chant of 'L – O – V – E. That spells LURVE!', following which the backing track kicks in. The jazzy ambience of 'In & Out Of Love' is maintained here, and it's now quite clear that it's down to the presence of Ciyo, who is a highly competent jazz guitarist in the mould of George Benson. It's a very sophisticated sound indeed, and the smooth close-harmony chorus that comes in soon afterwards can only enhance that. Each line consists of the whole group singing 'Love is...', followed by a response that says precisely what it is (sharing, caring, laughter etc.)

Each of these response lines is sung by a different member of the group, starting with Dennis himself, if I'm not mistaken. All four have very distinctive voices, which blend together very well. After this opening chorus, the four members take it in turn to sing a line of the verse, again starting with Dennis, who proclaims that it's a 'wonderful feeling that grows and grows.' This is a massively seductive song, in fact, and I can imagine that in another world, the lads could have been subjected to Take That levels of attention from the laydeez. Perhaps they were anyway. The fuller version of the main chorus that follows is interesting, because the chord sequence steps completely out of the world of reggae into late-night jazz, again one assumes thanks to the presence of Ciyo. The B side, 'The Essence of Love' is a kind of dub of 'Love Is...', except it's far too smooth really to qualify as anything so vulgar. All in all, this is an exceptionally classy package.

Four In A Row's only other single is 'Crazy Kind Of Love', also on Discotex records, 12", catalogue number DT20. The line up remains the same, even if Dennis' first name is spelt with only one n on the black and white picture sleeve (thank you once again, Mr Nero), which does perhaps give the enterprise a touch of French, or at least Blondie, ambience. Oh, Denis, oo-be-doo indeed. The title 'Crazy Kind Of Love' is rendered in a slightly wacky font at the top, and the main picture shows the four members of the group dressed in some quite extraordinarily shiny suits, adopting a pose involving awkwardly splayed legs and jazz hands. Once again, only Pinnock and Dawkins really carry it off.

On the back sleeve, they return to the more sober attire of their earlier photo shoot – actually, let's face it, it's probably from the same photo shoot as it's credited to Dan Harriot again – with a more clustered look. Pinnock and Dawkins are seated, looking reflective, whilst the other guys stand and sort of lean on them. Once again, the credits are thorough and feature a similar cast of thousands as last time. The DX7 has, however, been ditched in favour of an 'emulator', played by Skully and Bubbler (who I can't help but feel must have featured in a rejected pilot for *The X-Files*). This emulator thingy also seems to provide the trombone part, although the rest of the newly-added horns seem to be real, involving Smack Williams on Tenor Sax and Tan Tan on Trumpet. Most importantly of all, the credits reveal that the suits are from S.W.J./Turnpike. I was briefly tempted to get one myself, but my search was fruitless.

This is another cool piece of jazzy reggae. It actually starts off with a bit of a bebop-style guitar solo courtesy of Ciyo, and then we're into the harmony chorus, which essentially states that it's a crazy kind of love, over and over again. Around the middle of the last of these, a lower voice starts with 'Oooooh', and then we're into the verse, sung solo. This describes how the subject of the song sometimes gives him the blues, but every time she cries on his shoulder, she blows his mind. And so on. There's actually quite an annoying electronic keyboard effect that's a bit like a calliope overlaying this, but we'll let that pass as it isn't used again. Anyway, the song motors along quite happily, alternating solo voices and choruses, until round about the three-minute mark when there's another bebop thing on the guitar, at which point everyone vocalises along with it. Frankly, apart from that keyboard lapse, this must be the coolest reggae record ever made, and the only reason it wasn't a massive hit is because it was ahead of its time. C'mon, Jamie Cullum, forget Miles Davis – this is what you should be playing.

The B side, 'A World Of Your Own', is, once again, a sub-dub mash-up of 'Crazy Kind Of Love'. Not particularly essential, but serviceable enough. And that was the end of *Four in a Row*. But Dennis hung around with Tex Johnson as a solo artist for a little longer, as we'll see shortly.

Snoopy Speaks!

Basildon is a bit like Stevenage, except with a slight Hollywood complex. By which I mean that as you approach it along the A127, shortly after circumnavigating the impressively-yet-inexplicably-titled Fortune of War Not-Quite-Roundabout-More-An-Exaggerated-Kink-In-The-Road, you are faced with the word BASILDON in five foot high individually-sculpted letters planted on the opposite side of the road. Apart from this mildly hubristic feature which was added to the local landscape in 2010, Basildon is essentially famous for two things: firstly by recording the first major swing to Margaret Thatcher's Tories in the 1979 by-election, and secondly by giving birth to the band Depeche Mode. Only one of these is a good thing, but I'll let you work out which for yourself.*

However, it turns out that this corner of Essex also gave birth to a lesser-known musical talent, one who – amongst many other things – played a significant role in the development of Dennis Pinnock's career. And his name is Paul Nagle, also known as Snoopy. I interviewed him in his living room, which boasts an impressive array of shelves full of 12" vinyl – a small fraction of his collection. I began by asking him how on earth he – a white kid from Basildon – got involved with the UK Lovers Rock scene.

Clue: it's not the first one.

In 1975, Snoopy was living and working in London, nurturing a fanatical love for the reggae music that was beginning to bubble up into the general consciousness. At that time, pretty much the only writer in the music press who was taking any of it seriously was Penny Reel a.k.a. Scotty Bennett, who wrote for the *New Musical Express*. Despite the name (which was actually pinched from a song title by Eric 'Monty' Morris – if you happen to have access to the Trojan Ska Volume 2 Box Set, it's track eleven on Disc Two, and great fun it is too), Penny is actually a bloke, although for quite some time I was convinced he was a woman.

Anyway, the 16-year-old Snoopy wrote to the *NME* letters page in response to one of Reel's articles and his youthful passion so impressed the features editor, Neil Spencer, that he asked Snoopy to get in touch. He did, and was taken on as a writer, with his first piece being a review of Aswad's first LP. Disarmingly, Snoopy admits that the piece was the ramblings of a 16-year-old, heavily tweaked by the legendary Charles Shaar Murray prior to publication, but he got paid for it and his career as a music journalist was off and running. The odd thing was, when he mentioned this, I suddenly remembered actually seeing his byline.

Interestingly, I too was writing to the *NME* letters page round about then, although my contributions were of a somewhat less serious nature. My first one went something like this:

Betcha won't print this letter upside down,
DORIS THE PELICAN,
Cambridge

Yes, the body of the letter was indeed written upside down. And no, they didn't. In fact they appended this:

Dead right, we won't mate. You call this a letter? – M.B.

Which only goes to show you should never encourage an

133

attention-seeker, because I soon produced a follow-up. For this one, I abandoned the meta approach and went for what I imagined was wit. I was half right:

I have just discovered that NME is pronounced 'Enema' in French. Does this explain a lot about French musical taste?
BORIS O'PELICAN,
Clare College,
Cambridge

This time there was no riposte from the letters editor, and soon after that I gave up. I am not proud of any of this, and if you wish to use it as a counter-example any time someone tries to tell you that the Oxbridge universities are full of the elite of British youth, you're quite welcome.

Meanwhile, the far more sensible Snoopy was consolidating his position as one of the two key writers about reggae in the UK, with Penny Reel as his mentor. He wrote a few more pieces for *NME*, but one day in Daddy Kool Records in the West End – which in the way of these things had pretty much become Snoopy's second home – he was introduced him to the editor of the new *Black Echoes* magazine and Penny Reel suggested they take him on. Later that year, Snoopy took over *Black Echoes'* singles review column and ran that for the next few years as well as compiling all the charts for them. The music industry had him on the hook, and little by little it was pulling him in.

Some time after that Snoopy found himself in Greensleeves Records in West Ealing picking up their chart return data when he bumped into the Jamaican singer Dennis Brown. It turned out that Castro Brown's (no relation) Morpheus label were intending to launch Dennis Brown's own DEB label in the UK and they wanted Snoopy to work for them on press and publicity.

Grabbing the chance to pitch himself into the thick of it, he worked for the Browns in Battersea for about a year before he began to feel uncomfortable about the way Castro Brown was running things and started to look for other opportunities.

While working for DEB, Snoopy was still writing for *Black Echoes* and in the course of this, round about 1978, he had made the acquaintance of Tyrone (who Snoopy knew by his real name of Barrington – or Barry – Rowe), who as we know was running Venture Records at the time. They got on well, so when Tyrone offered him a job there, he crossed over the river and began working for him in Kensal Green, initially in publicity and promotion. However, Tyrone quickly realised that Snoopy could sing as well, so his job description was expanded to include vocal coach for Venture's bands.

About this time, Snoopy's own recording career got going, sort of. Tyrone's former protégées, Tradition (who we'll recall were Dennis Pinnock's backing band on his initial Venture release 'Ride On') had by now walked away from Tyrone and Venture and signed to RCA, who didn't have much of a clue what to do with them. Somehow, Snoopy managed to blag himself a session with RCA and recorded a single, the A side of which was a 'horrendous' reggae version of Lennon and McCartney's 'This Boy'. The B side was a cover of Heatwave's 'Mind Blowing Decisions', which was riding high in the charts at the time. Apparently, his rendition of it so impressed one of the members of Tradition who happened to be there at the time that he quickly recorded his own version, with the inevitable consequence that Snoopy's own single was ditched.

In case you're wondering which member of Tradition that was (because it's slightly relevant), Snoopy mentioned later on in our conversation that it was in fact Paul Dawkins, who recorded the song in conjunction with his band The Heptics, some years before he eventually hooked up with Dennis Pinnock in Four In

A Row. Reggae was indeed a small world in those days, and a cut-throat one too. However, somehow Snoopy had found himself at the heart of it all – particularly in the area of Lovers Rock, where he became one of its major champions.

When he met Dennis Pinnock in 1978, Dennis had already brought out 'Ride On' and 'Dennis the Menace' for Venture Records (indeed, Snoopy had reviewed them for *Black Echoes*). Their first task together was to choose songs for Dennis' putative album, which they began work on at Village Way Studios, Harrow in 1979, in sessions that went on until the early hours of the morning. During one of these sessions, Snoopy began to sing along various lyrics from the hits of the moment to one of the backing tracks they'd laid down, and then Dennis White, who worked at Gangsterville records and also happened to be there at the time, said to him why don't you record it as a medley?

So Snoopy went away with the backing track and began to choose the individual songs with the idea that he, Dennis Pinnock and Tyrone would record it, as Eargasm. Then they went back into the studio and what was to become 'This Is Lovers Rock' began to take shape, in one of those sessions where everything comes together and a kind of magic happens – even if they found that the medley went on for so long that they had to splice and re-use the rhythm track, with the result that it actually changes speed ever so slightly in the middle (it's OK, I hadn't spotted it). They got as far as recording guide vocals and sorting out all the harmonies, as well as the late-night arsing about that would eventually lead to P Pop and the Beagle's 'Name That Tune' (and Snoopy owned up to being 'The Beagle', with Dennis' alter ego being 'P Pop'). However, as they were working on the record, Snoopy's and Dennis' relationship with Tyrone began to unravel as it began to become apparent that they weren't seeing quite as much of the money as perhaps they had been led to expect.

The story of the music industry, especially in its early years and most especially in the reggae sector, is one of exploitation of artists by producers and label-owners. Snoopy's definitive comment to me was that he'd never met an honest person in the reggae business who was running a record label. At all. Not one. There wasn't one. The musicians and singers were fine, but the producers wanted everything for nothing.

Listening to Snoopy, I recalled a profile of Eddy Grant in *Time Out* magazine back in the late 70s, just before his major chart successes, which noted that he'd essentially taken control of every single stage of the production process for his own records, and it's blindingly obvious in retrospect why he did this. However, he was one of the lucky ones who had the necessary extra-musical skills to do this. Most of the other artists in the reggae industry didn't.

After the split, Tyrone put out a rough demo mix of 'This is Lovers Rock', initially on cassette, and it went straight to number one in the reggae charts without touching the sides. So in February 1980, Snoopy got a call from Tyrone:

'Hey, we've got a number one record!'

'Um, what record?'

'Y'know, that 'This Is Lovers Rock' thing. I put it out and it's gone straight to number one.'

(Speechless)

'Can you come and do some, um, PAs?'

I'm guessing Snoopy's response may well have been less diplomatic than the description of the conversation that he gave to me and may well have involved suggestions that Tyrone could go forth and multiply. After all, he hadn't even received a copy of the record, and besides at that time he was heavily involved in setting up a new reggae magazine called *Seen*. He'd got together with the accountant from Venture records, got a couple of designer friends in, rented offices in Edgware Road and got hold of Dennis Brown for a photoshoot for the first cover. However, even with advance orders for 40000 copies (which would, incidentally, have given it a circulation of approximately double that of *New Musical Express* in February 2014), the money men pulled the funds before they could even print a single edition.

But Tyrone was persuasive. He came around to Edgware Road and convinced Snoopy that they could all make up and be friendly again. So he started to put together a list of songs for a potential album and helped with promoting the single, which had now already spent four weeks at number one and was showing no signs of slowing down. Meanwhile, Island Records had got involved with distribution, bringing out a 7" version which was played on Capital a few times. There was even a whole page spread in the June 1980 edition of *Black Music* magazine and a photoshoot with pictures by Errol White, the drummer from Elements (and also, incidentally, the brother of Dennis 'Gangsterville' White – what did I say about the Lovers Rock family tree being just a tad complicated?)

That *Black Music* article, which has the excellent headline of 'Barbershop Breakthrough', is actually full of unrealised ambition, with talk of a forthcoming EP called 'Ear Games' in July of that year, featuring songs by Paul McCartney, Manhattan Transfer and Carole King, along with a 'four-part sub-"barbershop" treatment of "Blue Moon" taking [the] prize for outrageous leftfield reggae.' I would so love to have heard that, as well as the album that they had planned for December, which was to feature Cole Porter and Burt Bacharach alongside Holland/Dozier/Holland. I would have also quite liked to have seen the stage show that they envisaged, described in that piece as 'a spectacle, with costume changes and the whole bit. Like Manhattan Transfer, for instance.' And why not?

But according to Snoopy, the money still wasn't forthcoming, so he decided enough was enough and called time on his relationship with Tyrone. And that was the last he saw of him. I would love to have been able to get Tyrone's side of the story, but sadly he provided impossible to track down, despite all my best efforts.

It was obvious from talking to Snoopy that he retains a massive amount of respect and affection for Dennis Pinnock. As he said, Dennis had a very distinctive and versatile voice. He was also a serious music fan with interests that stretched far beyond the narrow confines of reggae, and I got the impression that Snoopy's as mystified as I am as to why he never broke through. When they were both involved with Venture they were obviously big buddies, often going to gigs and house parties together, but when I first called Snoopy, he'd lost touch with him since the early 80s. However, by the time I actually met him, he'd hooked up with Dennis on Facebook, so at least I could say that I'd played a part in reuniting two-thirds of Eargasm. It's not quite the same as getting The Beatles back together, but I still think it's quite nice.

After Eargasm and the *Seen* debacle, Snoopy had a brief period working at Cavalis records along with a couple of the guys from Matumbi, although in the grand reggae tradition this did not end well – possibly owing to the fact that it was run by a couple of white guys whose previous experience in business was limited to selling double glazing. He also put together a new Eargasm line-up to record 'This Is Lovers Rock Too' in 1984, but that failed to achieve the same level of success as the first one. Snoopy left the reggae world soon afterwards, partly because he was just wanted to try something different but mainly because, as he put it to me, he was sick of being ripped off and exploited by whoever he worked for.

So Snoopy ended up managing a record shop for the rest of the 20th century, before switching careers again to become Reader in Residence in Essex – which sounds the best job ever, as it basically involved encouraging people to read books. After a stint as Community Arts Director for a local school, he set up The Smile Group with his business partner, where they provide a range of training and coaching services.

And then one day, Castro Brown got in touch with him out of the blue to ask him to accept an award for his services to Lovers Rock at the 2008 Reggae Awards. That led to him meeting Penny Reel again as well as Menelik Shabazz, which in turn led to him appearing in the documentary, which is ultimately what brought me to his door.

One final thing. Just what *were* all those songs on 'This Is Lovers Rock'? Here's Snoopy's definitive list:

IT'S YOU I LOVE (originally by Jamaican group The Techniques - 1968) Lead: Tyrone

SOON FORWARD (originally by Gregory Isaacs - 1979) Lead: Snoopy

THIS IS LOVERS ROCK (I created the interludes throughout the song - 1979) Lead: Dennis

LOVE THE WAY IT SHOULD BE (originally by The Royal Rasses - 1975) Lead: Dennis

BREEZIN' (originally by Tradition - 1978) Lead: Tyrone

THIS IS LOVERS ROCK - Lead: Dennis

SWEET FEELINGS (originally by The Abysinnians - 1976) Lead: Snoopy

I'M SO PROUD (originally by American group The Impressions - 1963) Lead: Tyrone

GROOVIN' (originally by The Young Rascals - 1967) Lead: Tyrone

RIVER JORDAN (originally by Sugar Minott – 1979) Lead: Dennis

POINT OF VIEW (originally by Matumbi - 1978) Lead: Snoopy

I'M JUST A GUY (originally by Alton Ellis - 1967) Lead: Dennis

THIS IS LOVERS ROCK - Lead: Dennis

EVERY LITTLE BEAT OF MY HEART (originally by Tradition - 1977) Lead: Tyrone

SITTING IN THE PARK (originally by soul singer Billy Stewart - 1965) Lead: Snoopy

WAITING IN THE PARK (originally The Chantells - 1977) Lead: Dennis

TELEPHONE LINE (originally by Tony J. - 1976) Lead: Snoopy

PICK UP THE PIECES (originally by The Royals - 1972) Lead: Tyrone

MY CONVERSATION (originally by The Uniques - 1968) Lead: Dennis

MOVIN' ON (originally by Tradition - 1977) Lead: Tyrone

THIS IS LOVERS ROCK - Lead: Tyrone

MR. BROWN (originally by Gregory Isaacs - 1979) Leads: Dennis, Snoopy and Tyrone

The Eargasm record is terrific, but it's also worth tracking down the originals of some of those songs. Frankly, the clue really is in the title of the medley: this *is* Lovers Rock.

My Life as a Rock God Oboist

By now I'm sure you're wondering if I've ever entertained notions of becoming a star in the music world myself. The answer is, of course, yes – why would anyone *not* want to become a rock star? – although it's not an ambition I've ever pursued with any great degree of commitment. However, I was in a band once. I really was.

The first thing I should say is that I've never learnt to play one of the musical instruments normally associated with rock'n'roll. After an unbelievably promising early career as a junior recorder prodigy, in the course of which I so outshone the rest of the class at that godawful trainer instrument that I was permitted to progress from tootling on my own bog standard descant model to borrowing teacher's treble, things went seriously downhill when I came to choose a proper instrument to study. The powers that be decided that the school orchestra needed more oboe players, so that's what my nine-year-old self got lumbered with. Not long afterwards, it became gruesomely apparent that my brilliant musical career had already peaked.

The thing about the oboe is that it's a double reed instrument. You get a noise by pinching the two halves together between your lips and blowing so as to make them vibrate. That causes a sympathetic vibration in the air column inside the instrument itself and … well, this isn't a physics book, so we won't go any further with that. Just believe me when I say it's a bloody awful struggle to get any noise out of the thing, let alone something approaching music. The first thing my parents asked my teacher when they met to discuss my progress was 'Is he supposed to turn that colour?'

In a more sensible age, I would have abandoned the whole stupid idea and tried something else, like the spoons perhaps, but in those days and in our household WE PINNOCKS DID NOT GIVE UP THINGS. We kept buggering on, and so I spent several more ghastly years fighting against the bastard. To be fair, it did introduce me to the joys of playing in various orchestras and ensembles (some of which even had GIRLS in them), but all along I was painfully aware of one thing. I had chosen to learn the least cool instrument on the planet.

Consider the facts. How many rock oboe riffs can you name? I'll tell you. There's just one, on Roxy Music's 'Virginia Plain'. The guy playing it, Andy Mackay, is undoubtedly cool (he was in Roxy Music, goddammit), but he's not an oboist. He's a saxophonist playing the oboe. Crucial difference: sax cool, oboe massively uncool. When Kingsley Amis wanted one of Jim Dixon's housemates, Evan Johns, to play an absurd musical instrument in 'Lucky Jim', what did he give him? I'll tell you. The oboe, that's what he gave him.

Does the instrument choose the person? Did I look like an oboe player in my nine-year-old shorts, knobbly knees and long socks? Did the world look at me and see 'Nope, he's not cool. Give him an oboe?' Did it simply reinforce an inherent uncoolness? I'll never know now; I am way past the age where coolness either matters or is possible. But it did matter once, which is probably why, when I went to university and I saw the notice advertising for people to join a spontaneous improvising ensemble, I thought it was worth a shot.

It was every bit as good and as bad as it sounds. We were a pretty mixed bunch. The de facto leader was a French horn player – another misfit. The French horn is at least a brass instrument, which elevates it above the woodwinds, but any instrument that you have to dismantle several times during a performance to drain out the collected saliva is massively lacking in sex appeal. There was also a violinist. Now that one can go either way, but this guy was definitely cool, because he was long-haired, good-looking and foreign. The line-up was completed by a rather staid bass-player, a pianist and a couple of saxophonists. The first of these was the guy who had circulated the original notice and was far too good for us, with the result that he disappeared pretty soon after the first session. The second one stuck around for a bit longer, which was a shame because he only knew one riff and he was damned sure he was going to work it into every single thing we played. Other folk drifted in and out as they pleased, adding to or subtracting from the quality as they did so.

The music was essentially the kind of stuff they take the piss out of in the Jazz Club sketches on The Fast Show ('Nice'): a bunch of guys in a room ineptly trying to take something they'd picked up on and do something new with it, or – more often – just blasting out something of their own instead in an attempt to dominate the proceedings. Every now and then something came together and we all seemed to be working with each other, but those moments were few and far between. I know this because, like Richard Nixon, we taped everything, so WE HAVE EVIDENCE. And, masochist that I am, I have listened to it all.

Oh yes, the name. We decided we needed a suitably wacky name, so someone came up with 'Misunderstood on the Way to Sainsbury's'. Then someone else pointed out that it would be really cool to, like, y'know, change the last word to Sanesberries, man, 'cos that shows how TOTALLY MENTAL we are. So that's how we ended up being called 'Misunderstood on the Way to Sanesberries'. Fortunately, we weren't ever called upon to use this name on the bill for a gig, because no-one ever actually asked us. We did, however, put on a free concert by ourselves, serendipitously choosing a night when the college rugby club were having a get-together in the bar next door, with the result that we had an audience of a sort drifting in and out of the room in an increasingly bemused state as the evening went on.

I would love to conclude this by saying something along the lines of '… but he went on to be one of the founder-members of The Teardrop Explodes', but as far as I'm aware none of us has ever done anything memorable musically in all the years since. However, the saxophonist who started it all and then cleared off did rise to become a British High Commissioner somewhere in Africa, though, so he obviously had the right idea.

There is an odd postscript to this, however. When I first moved to London, I rented a flat in Streatham and I tried to set up an improvising group myself, putting a card on the notice board in the local independent bookshop. I got one reply, from a rather introverted singer-songwriter, who was living over in Clapham at the time. I went to visit him, listened to him singing some of his songs and decided he was, frankly, a bit of a loser, and the idea of the improvising ensemble was swiftly abandoned. A few years back, I happened across the note he'd written to me in response to my card and noticed the signature: John Hegley. To think I could have been one of the original Popticians if I'd played my cards right.

An Intrusive Organ

After Four In A Row went their separate ways, Dennis Pinnock's next solo offering was 'Reconsider Me' (Discotex Records 12", catalogue number DT22). The budget doesn't seem to have stretched to a picture sleeve this time, so we don't have quite so much to go on for the credits. Both 'Reconsider Me' and the B side, 'Let's Reconcile', are credited to Dennis Pinnock as sole writer. Both sides are tersely described as 'Arr. & Prod. By Ciyo for DiscoTex Productions', and the record is 'Mktd. By DiscoTex Records' and 'Pub. By DiscoTex Music'. You certainly can't accuse Discotex of profligacy with ink.

I'm in two minds about the music. It's a bouncy uptempo number with the kind of jazzy feel that we'd be expecting from Ciyo. There are some exquisite vocals from Dennis and some typically lovely close harmony from his backing singers (who I'm guessing may well have included most of *Four In A Row*). The lyrics are poignant, if unexceptional:

> *Please reconsider me,*
> *Girl, let's reconcile.*
> *Please reconsider me,*
> *Won't you change your mind?*
>
> *I didn't mean to hurt you so…*
> etc. etc..

But. But but but but but. The accompaniment has a heavily-featured Hammond Organ. Now in the right hands, a Hammond – like any organ – can be a wonderful thing, particularly in the realm of jazz. You only have to think of Jimmy 'The Cat' Smith or Booker T. Jones (by the way, did you know that his middle name is just T? Isn't that amazingly cool?). But the problem is that the Hammond Organ pretty much defines that area on the musical Venn diagram where 'Cool' overlaps with 'Cheese'. And the Hammond on 'Reconsider Me' is as cheesy as a half-pound of finest Stinking Bishop. Frankly, this track wouldn't sound out of place on Radio 2's 'The Organist Entertains' – and if ever there was a title that was diametrically opposed to the content of a programme, it's that one. Not good at all.

Worse than that, the B side is basically exactly the same thing without Dennis' vocals on top, which is as good a definition of subtraction of value as you're likely to come across. Now if on the other hand you were to take away that organ, we'd be making progress. Dear oh dear.

The good news is that Dennis' next record, 'Woman Be Fair', (Discotex Records 12", catalogue number DT24) is a bit of a return to form. Ciyo's jazzy inflections have been dropped in favour of a return to reggae basics. Writing credits go to Tex Johnson himself and it's written, arranged and produced by Tex Johnson for Discotex productions, assisted by Spy and Steel, and mixed at Ariwa by Mad Proffessor (sic). Mysteriously the capital T in the middle of Discotex has reverted to lower case and the passing abbreviation fad has also run its course.

Hold on a moment. Mad Professor? THE Mad Professor? The Mad Professor who's collaborated with Lee 'Scratch' Perry on no less than TEN albums as well as working with pretty much everyone else under the sun including – them again! – Massive Attack? Well, if it was done at Ariwa Studios, it most certainly was, because that's the Mad Prof's place of business. Wow. Add one more notch to Mr Pinnock's bedpost.

The lyrics are essentially a plea for the singer's paramour to exhibit some consistency and say definitively either that she does or doesn't, and also whether she ultimately will or won't. The precise activity under discussion is not revealed, but I think we can probably hazard a guess. This isn't a bad record at all – nicely wistful in tone and the production is pretty sharp too, apart from a very eighties ascending synthesizer chord sequence that bursts in at the lead-up to the chorus. The other thing that sticks out is a jolly little counterpoint played on a synth that sounds a bit like a celeste, and it nags away at you for ages before you realise that it's almost the exact same tune used in Van McCoy's seventies disco smash, 'Do The Hustle'. Which is unexpected, to say the least. Still, this is a record that could have done pretty well for itself with a bit of airplay on the likes of Capital Radio.

The B side, 'Fair's Fair', is not – to my great disappointment – the demented freakout that I'd been hoping for. Instead, it's a sort of half-hearted dub, with Dennis' vocal stripped away once more and the occasional spot of reverb echo added. I do get the feeling that Tex Johnson wasn't as much of a fan of Le Dub as Tyrone, more's the pity, and even the presence of the Mad Professor doesn't seem to have added much to the mix.

Dennis' next recording for Tex is actually really interesting, because it takes him to a place where, in a different life, he could so easily have built his entire career . Because there are no two ways about it. 'So In Love' (Discotex 12", catalogue number DT28) is a *soul* record. Unusually for Dennis, it's a cover – of a song by Leroy Hutson dating back to 1973. I'd never actually heard of Hutson prior to this, but it turns out that he took Curtis Mayfield's place as lead singer of The Impressions after the latter left, staying with them for two and a half years. I felt a bit better about not having heard of him after reading that he was also known as the 'best-kept secret of Seventies Soul'. So, basically soul's equivalent of Dennis Pinnock, then.

This is the only one of Dennis' records that doesn't start with a drum flourish. Not only that, but most of the accompaniment is squarely on the beat, with the understated keyboards being the only concession to reggae whatsoever. It's actually rather lovely, with a flutey organ descant that harks back to the late sixties, and an occasional jazzy chorus crooning 'So in love' from time to time. This may well be the best solo record that Dennis produced during his time with Tex Johnson – in fact I'd put it near the top of his complete output.

The B side is – sigh – another oddity. It's attributed to the Disco Tex Band, and Dennis doesn't appear to take any part in it at all. The piece is an instrumental entitled 'Steel Pan Rocksteady', and it is indeed a gently lilting reggae tune with added steel drums. Musically, it is entirely unremarkable, and the only remotely interesting thing about it is that it's quite rare to find the combination of music from both ends of the West Indies. Then again, Kingston and Port of Spain are over 1100 miles away from each other – about as far away as Minsk is from London – so maybe it's not that surprising.

And with that, it seems as if Dennis and Tex Johnson parted company for a while, although they would get back together for a few more recordings in the nineties. However, the next thing that Dennis did was an even more unexpected collaboration.

'White Hat' SEO and
Other Search Strategies

The excitement of having actually secured an interview with someone who had actually once worked with Dennis Pinnock slowly dissipated over the following days as it became all too evident that my quest to speak to the man himself was still progressing at the rate of treacle flowing up a slope made of loose shale. Obviously I messaged Dennis again, hoping that the fact that we now had a Facebook friend in common might help in this regard:

Hello again,

Had a great time yesterday chatting to Snoopy. Believe you're in contact with him again. Would really appreciate talking to you as well. Check with him if you like - I'm quite harmless.

Maybe the smiley face I added at the end was a bit twee. Either way, it didn't exactly propel him into action. So I had another look around to see who else I could pin down.

According to his Facebook profile, Tex Johnson was now the managing director of a web design company called Top Rank Media. A search for references to that threw up a post about it from 2009 on a site called PRWEB under the tagline 'SEO Consultant Top Rank Web Designs Gives Away 250 Free Websites'. I lost interest in the piece, along with – temporarily – the will to live, when it started banging on about stuff like 'using strictly "white hat" SEO strategies', but before I did so I noticed that alongside the piece there was a phone number and what purported to be a link to Tex's company's web site. However, the latter turned out to be to an unregistered domain and the former just rang and rang when I tried it. By this time, I have to say I wasn't in the least bit surprised.

Despite the fact that the only message I was getting from Facebook was that messaging strangers was a waste of time, I went back to searching friend lists, and found Tony Nero, the graphic artist who had worked on the covers for 'Ride On' and the ones for *Four In A Row*. Setting aside my issues with someone who managed to misspell both Dennis' surname (on 'Ride On') and first name (on 'Crazy Kind Of Love'), I sent him a message:

Hi,

This is going to sound more than a little weird and random, but here goes. Basically, I'm writing a book inspired by coming across a record by my namesake Dennis Pinnock, and I'm trying to talk to anyone who had anything to do with him, however tangentially.

I've already had a very interesting chat with Snoopy, who sang with him in Eargasm. I'm guessing you're the guy who did the graphics for both the 'Ride On' sleeve and the two Four In A Row sleeves.

Would you be prepared to answer a few questions?

I also tried Paul Dawkins of *Four In A Row*, asking him pretty much the same thing, adding – quite truthfully – that I loved those FIAR records in case that added any extra weight. But once again it seemed that neither Tony nor Paul were going to play ball with me.

I even tried Ariwa Studios, home of The Mad Professor:

Bit of a long shot, I'm doing some research for a book and I noticed that the Mad Professor is listed as having mixed a record by Dennis Pinnock called 'Woman Be Fair'. I'm guessing it was back in the late 80s, and it was on Discotex Records, catalogue no DT24. Do you happen to have any more information about that session? Did the Mad Professor do much other work for Tex Johnson?

Many thanks in advance for any information you can provide.

Much to my surprise, Holly Fraser at Ariwa Studios did get back in touch very quickly, but wasn't able to shed any more light. She agreed that it was very likely that such a session did take place as Mad Professor did indeed work with Tex Johnson around that time. However, it was all too long ago to locate any more information. Which was all fair enough, I guess; it *was* all a long time ago – a long undocumented time ago. And that made me think a bit about the real reason why no-one was interested in talking. It's entirely possible that the whole idea of writing a book about reggae – and particularly as obscure a corner of it as this one – simply didn't make sense to them. If you believe Frank Zappa's dictum that writing about music is like dancing about architecture*, you'd struggle to find an endeavour that was more pointless than writing about a musical genre that's as physical in nature as reggae.

I'm reluctant to introduce cultural bias here, but I do wonder if that's why, as Snoopy said to me, pretty much everyone who wrote about reggae in the early days was white – and there weren't even that many of them. Perhaps only a white person would be daft enough to miss the point to the extent that they wanted to write about it instead of dancing to it. If you set aside the lakes of ink that have been expended on the life and work of Bob Marley, reggae is singularly under-represented on the world's bookshelves, and the whole of the Lovers Rock scene is damn nearly invisible. Search for 'Lovers Rock' on Amazon, and all you'll find that's remotely relevant is a bunch of dodgy efforts stitched together from Wikipedia. So I do hope you appreciate what an important book you're reading here.

---

* And, yes, I know it's been ascribed to several thousand other folk as well, but I'm going with Zappa simply because it sounds like it ought to be one of his.

The odd thing is that – along with my hopeless ambition to be a rock'n'roll God – I did once harbour ambitions to be a music journalist. I'd suppressed this to a large extent, but one or two memories bubbled up after meeting Snoopy. You see, it could almost have been me.

In 1976, the year after Snoopy started working for them, the *New Musical Express* ran a competition to attract more new writing talent – the key phrase they used was 'hip young gunslingers'. The touchingly old-fashioned task set was to write a review of your favourite album, and the two chosen were – famously – Julie Burchill and Tony Parsons. Typically, Burchill hit the zeitgeist firmly on the nose by writing a review of Patti Smith's 'Horses'. My submission, however, was so way off and uncool that it wouldn't have even known how to spell the word zeitgeist. I can barely bring myself to admit it, but the truth is that the album I chose to review was 'Tales of Topographic Oceans' by Yes, an album so pretentiously prog you could feed it to a family of elves and keep them alive for a week. I think I even used the word 'gamelan' at one point. I stood about as much chance of being taken on by *NME* as Eddie the Eagle would have had of getting a job as the editor of The International Journal of Ski Jumping.

Having said that, if I'd actually announced that I intended to abandon my studies and work in music journalism, I guess my parents would have responded in the same way as if I'd announced my intention to seek my fortune as a rent boy. So perhaps it was all for the best. And yet…

Dog-Face Phil's Slaves

I needed to know exactly how involved Philip Pinnock was in the slavery game. In some ways it scarcely mattered whether he just owned a handful or a whole army of them – either way, it was an unspeakably evil business – but nonetheless I wanted to get some idea of the scale of it all.

It's a curious thing, but it so often happens that when supposedly civilised people get involved in atrocities like the slave trade (or, indeed, the Holocaust), they are utterly meticulous about recording the details of what they have done. Maybe they feel that by writing it all down in an official-looking record, rather than being secretive about it all, it somehow legitimises the venture. What this means is that we can in fact say precisely how many slaves there were in Jamaica at various times during the eighteenth century. By apportioning that according to the relative size of Philip Pinnock's land, I reckoned I could get a feel for how many of them he owned.

I based the data for land ownership on the Quit Rent books kept by the Jamaican government; Quit Rent was essentially a sort of taxation based on how much land you owned. Fortunately, someone had already transcribed this data for one year and put it up on the Jamaican Family Search website, so that was my next port of call.

In 1754, the year for which land data is available (and coincidentally the year in which he was appointed to the position of Chief Justice), Philip Pinnock seems to have owned a total of

3977 acres (2886 in St Andrew, 755 in St Thomas in the East, 276 in St George and 60 in St Ann). But wait, what's this? Thomas Pinnock, his less vocal elder brother, also seems to have been quietly amassing his own property portfolio, with a total of 4713 acres to his name (1099 in St Andrew, 2924 in St Thomas in the East and 690 in Westmoreland). We might as well add their combined land together, as they're all in the same family. This gives us a grand total of 8690 acres belonging to the Pinnock brothers. Finally, there's a further 985 jointly held by Philip Pinnock and another chap called Richard Swarten, so we'll chuck that into the mix as well, making 9675 acres in all.

Now for the tricky task of adding up all the rest. I'll be back in a few minutes…

OK, I'm back. I make the total land owned by all the planters in Jamaica at that time to be somewhere in the region of 1.66 million acres. And just to check, that's around 2600 square miles, which is in the right ballpark, because the total area of the Jamaican land mass is 4243 square miles. Phew. So that means that the Pinnock brothers owned roughly 0.0058 – just over half a percent – of Jamaica's plantable area.

Now let's look at the other side of the calculation. Whilst we have detailed information on the numbers of slaves imported to and exported from Jamaica (and there actually seems to have been a fair amount of two-way traffic between Jamaica and elsewhere, presumably because they were as much of a tradeable commodity as anything else), data on slave deaths is less easy to find. Actual figures of slave populations are only available for a number of specific years in the 18th century: 1734 (when there were 86546 slaves for 7644 whites), 1739 (99239 slaves for 10080 whites), 1745 (112428 slaves for 11330 whites), 1761 (146000 slaves for 15330 whites) and 1768 (166904 slaves and 17000 whites). Just to put that in perspective, UK readers may like to know that the 1768 slave population is just under the entire population of Bournemouth recorded in the 2001 census.

For the purposes of this calculation, let's go with that 1768 figure, as it probably represents the situation when Philip Pinnock was at his peak earning power. We'll also assume that the land proportion owned by him and his brother is the same as in 1754, although chances are that given his position within the Jamaican establishment, he had probably had more than one opportunity to add to his acreage, especially when one considers that he eventually amassed enough money to buy that stonking great £25000 mansion.

To get a crude estimate of the number of slaves owned by the Pinnocks, it's probably not unreasonable to assume that the 166904 were spread pretty evenly over the owned land, although I'm guessing that the 61 acres in St Catherine owned by 'Morris, William a free Negro' should strictly speaking be excluded from the calculation. So on that basis, it looks like between them they would have owned a little under 1000 slaves, of which around half would have belonged to Philip. Whichever way you look at it, that's a hell of a lot of men's souls to have absolute dominion over.

Those slave population figures, incidentally, come from Edward Long's 1774 book *THE HISTORY OF JAMAICA. OR, GENERAL SURVEY OF THE ANTIENT AND MODERN STATE OF THAT ISLAND WITH Reflections on its Situation, Settlements, Inhabitants, Climate, Products, Commerce, Laws, and Government.* This is, frankly, a pretty hideous book to read, as the author is – as James Walvin's *A Short History of Slavery* sardonically puts it – 'no friend to the slaves'. Long was a member of a well-established planter family (that 1754 land list mentions both Samuel and Charles of that ilk, with 6755 and 3087 acres to their names respectively), although he himself was only in Jamaica from 1757 to 1769, during which time he was an enthusiastic planter and slave-owner himself. In his book, he certainly comes over as a virulent pro-slavery campaigner, at least when he isn't making stereotypical anti-semitic remarks about the local Jewish population. For example, on p267 of Book II:

> *The planters of this island have been very unjustly stigmatized with an accusation of treating their Negroes with barbarity. Some alledge (sic), that the slave-holders (as they are pleased to call them, in contempt) are lawless bashaws, West-India tyrants, inhuman oppressors, bloody inquisitors, and a long, &c. of such pretty names.*

Well yes. But Long goes on to say:

> *The planter, in reply to these bitter invectives, will think it sufficient to urge, in the first place, that he did not make them slaves, but succeeded to the inheritance of their services in the same manner as an English squire succeeds to the estate of his ancestors; and that, as to his Africans, he buys their services from those who have all along pretended a very good right to sell; that it cannot be in his interest to treat his Negroes in the manner represented; but it is so to use them well, and preserve their vigour and existence as long as he is able. [rambles on in this vein for several more pages – JP]*

So that's all right, then. But it gets worse, far worse. Later on in the book, we enter much dodgier territory when on page 336 we read this:

> *For my own part, I think there are extremely potent reasons for believing, that the White and the Negroe [sic] are two distinct species. A certain philosopher of the present age confidently avers, that 'none but the blind can doubt it'. It is certain, that this idea enables us to account for those diversities of feature, skin, and intellect, observeable among*

mankind; which cannot be accounted for in any other way,
without running into a thousand absurdities.'

For some reason, Long decides not to pursue this any further until a stray neuron fires round about page 351 and he begins a chapter with the title 'Negroes', in which he lays out his thesis in extraordinary and breathtakingly racist detail, at which point we are minded to hurl the book into the fire. This so-called history of Long's was a significant weapon in the attack on the burgeoning abolitionist movement and it's well worth a look if you want to get inside the mentality of the slave-owners and how they tried to justify their position from an intellectual standpoint.

By an odd coincidence, the entry on Edward Long in Frank Cundall's *Biographical Annals of Jamaica* appears directly after the one for Philip Pinnock. Long's history was written only a few years after a time when Dog-Face Phil was Chief Justice of Jamaica, in charge of a penal code, the unrepealed third clause of which, as described by Long, stated that a slave found in possession of stolen goods would, at the discretion of two justices and three freeholders, 'suffer death, transportation, dismembering, or other punishment'. Amusingly, Long adds a footnote to this stating that 'this inhuman penalty [dismembering] is entirely obsolete, and never of late inflicted', while saying nothing about the alternative penalty of death.

All this happened a long time ago, in a different world with a different moral code. Obviously, that doesn't make it right, but I wonder if I can truly put my hand on my heart and say I wouldn't have behaved in exactly the same way if I'd been put in the same position in the same culture as my namesake and presented with the same opportunities for my own betterment. Sugar production in Jamaica was after all a truly massive industry, with a workforce equivalent to the massed ranks of present-day ExxonMobil and BP combined. I'd like to think that I'd have been one of the good guys like Wilberforce – of course I do! – but that would have involved swimming against some pretty fierce tides.

What we can say with some conviction is that Philip Pinnock himself would have had no interest whatsoever in engaging in any such contraflow men's freestyle. The fact is, he was heavily involved in the slavery business. Indeed, we can be pretty certain he was in it up to his neck.

Sugaring the Pill

As the eighties drew to a close, Dennis' career seems to be starting to fragment. The next disc he appeared on was a 12" on Up Tempo records, catalogue number TEMP 028. Actually dating this one proved to be a bit tricky, but I managed to establish that it was later than 1988 (because Tapir's online discography gives that year for TEMP 023 – Jack Wilson's version of Breakfast In Bed c/w Never Gonna Give You Up, in case you're interested, and why wouldn't you be) and earlier than May 1990 (because the phone number for Jetstar distribution given on the label is a London 01 number and that's when the 01 numbers split into 071 and 081).

The really curious thing about this record is that it has Dennis on Side A, with a song called 'Drifting Away' and none other than Sugar Minott on Side AA, with a song called 'Drifter'. There's no clue as to whether Side A outranks Side AA (although curiously on eBay, sellers tend to refer to Side AA as the B side), but there's no doubt as to which of the two singers had a higher profile and it most certainly wasn't Dennis Pinnock.

Lincoln Barrington 'Sugar' Minott (1956 – 2010) was one of the first Jamaica-based reggae singers to see the potential of Lovers Rock, relocating to the UK in 1980 just before his massive hit 'Good Thing Going', which reached number 4 in the UK singles chart. More recently he also appeared as one of the Easy Star All Stars on their wonderful 'Radiodread' album, which is exactly what it sounds like – a collection of reggae covers of Radiohead songs. That alone gives him several zillion cool points in my book. But how on earth did he end up sharing a disc with

Dennis Pinnock (incidentally, one that doesn't appear in any of his discographies), other than the similarity of the two songs' titles?

We'll come onto the possible reasons behind this later, but first of all, we need to take a listen to the music. The writer of the song isn't credited – unless they really have changed their name to 'Adapted' – which isn't a promising start. It's arranged and produced by Steven King (no, not that one) and mixed by Dennis and MADLA (sic). A brief search throws up several possibilities for songs by other artists entitled 'Drifting Away', including Faithless, Roy Orbison and – a new one on me – Doug and the Slugs, but none of these seems to be the original template for Pinnock's song. MADLA is equally mysterious, it being unlikely that this is a reference to the eponymous district of Stavanger.

But is it any good? Oh dear. Oh dear oh dear oh dear. This could have been a lovely record, it really could. There's a nice lilting Latin beat to it, another fine vocal performance from Dennis and some really nice close-harmony backing vocals, but the whole thing is destroyed – and I mean utterly wrecked, demolished and obliterated beyond recognition using anything other than dental records – by the crassest drum machine you will ever hear in your life. This horrific cybernetic automaton gets switched on at the beginning of the record and bashes on with the same dum-de-dum da dum-de-dum da-da rhythm over and over again, high up at the top end of the mix, right through to the end. There are six minutes and fourteen seconds of this, and it will be six minutes and fourteen seconds of your life that you will want returned to you with interest after you have finished. Sadly, however, they are six minutes and fourteen seconds of your life that have gone forever.

So how did this monstrosity come to end up on the flipside of a Sugar Minott record? As far as I can tell, Minott was co-owner of Up Tempo records with Steven King and for him it was a useful vehicle for re-distributing tunes that he'd liberated from Studio One following his acrimonious split with them.

Up Tempo records seem to be still in existence, with a web site and everything, even if Steven King was in fact listed as *Stephen* King on the 'About' page. Unfortunately it wasn't entirely clear how to contact them, as there was no e-mail address listed. However, I had a brilliant inspiration. They had an online shop. With PayPal. All I had to do was buy something and that would give me access to their e-mail address! To this day, I'm not really sure what I bought. I think it may have been a Sugar Minott MP3 of some sort, but as it hasn't arrived through the post yet I could be wrong. Still, it was less than a quid and as a result I did indeed get an e-mail address that looked promising. So I duly got in touch and asked them if they could give me any information about Dennis and how he ended up on that Sugar Minott B side, why that record didn't appear in Minott's discography and was Minott involved with the running of Up Tempo?

I didn't hear anything from them.

However, I still wasn't defeated, because on one of the pages of the Up Tempo site, it gave the name of their website designer. I Googled the name and the very first hit was for a website designer specialising in small businesses. I e-mailed him and he actually got back to me, agreeing to pass my query on. But once again there was no reply, so I abandoned that line of enquiry. The Sugar Minott connection would have to remain a mystery.

The Penultimate Domino

At this point in my quest, I was developing a vision that everything should somehow lead up to a grand, emotional meeting with Dennis Pinnock. However, despite everything, it still seemed entirely possible that I would fail. Now I could ask Snoopy to broker the encounter, but I didn't really want to do it that way for a number of reasons. First of all, it seemed a bit like cheating. Secondly, I really did want to speak to some of the other guys who had worked with him first. And thirdly, it seemed a bit off, now that they were back in touch again for the first time in thirty years, to try and make capital out of it.

So I went back to my social network stalking. First of all, I pestered Tex Johnson on Facebook again, this time pointing out that if and when the book came out, there would obviously be considerable interest in those old recordings of Dennis and *Four In A Row*, to which presumably he still had the rights. But even that didn't have any effect. I also tried Ciyo Brown again, both via Facebook and via the message box on his website, but that didn't work either. Menelik Shabazz – who I now had two friends in common thanks to my connection with Snoopy – remained equally uninterested. I even tried messaging Dennis Bovell, just because he seemed a nice bloke on both the Shabazz documentary and the BBC's 'Reggae Britannia'. OK, I admit that was a bit random and in any case there was no dice there either.

I also sent a message to 'British Lovers Rock Music' on Myspace, on the basis that it was almost certainly Tyrone himself behind the account. Again, I pointed out the likely potential interest in the old Venture recordings when the book was published, but I didn't hold out much hope there either as the account hadn't been accessed since 2010. Finally, I located an e-mail address for the legendary Penny Reel himself and pinged him, but once more I found myself pissing into the proverbial wind.

Most of the record labels that Dennis had been involved with were now defunct, but there were a couple that seemed to be contactable. Joe G's in particular had an online presence, and were actually offering an MP3 of 'Slice of Life' for sale on their site. Not only that, but they had an e-mail address, so I got in touch:

Hi,

I just got hold of a copy of Dennis Pinnock's 'Slice of Life' on vinyl, and I was wondering if you could tell me anything about when it was recorded? I'm actually writing a book based around the fact that Dennis and I share the same surname, and I would be very interested in interviewing anyone involved - would you be prepared to help? (I haven't managed to talk to Dennis himself yet, although I have spoken to Snoopy, who once worked with him.)

I notice that you have MP3's of the song for sale on your site - I would anticipate some increased sales if and when the book comes out!

A couple of weeks later, they replied back, saying that they were unable to help me and that I should contact Mr Pinnock directly for the information that I needed for my book. At which point I smacked my head and said to myself, why didn't I think of that? To be fair, they did also give me a link to his Facebook page as well as what appeared to be a completely different Dennis Pinnock's Myspace, but it wasn't quite the leg up I'd been hoping for.

I'd also been wondering if it might be worth trying to have a chat with someone at Jet Star Records, who seemed to handle the distribution on a fair percentage of Dennis' records. It would at least be interesting to talk to someone about the various label bosses they came into contact with. However, Jet Star went into administration in 2008 and the name, along with the extensive associated back catalogue, was subsequently bought up by Phoenix Music International. I gave them a call just on the off chance, but it turned out that they hadn't actually taken on any of the old Jet Star employees. But they did say that the old Jet Star was still operational, under the name Jet Star Digital.

Jet Star Digital proved a bit harder to make contact with. It was easy enough to find their company details, along with the address where the company was registered. But there was no e-mail address or phone number – or indeed website. How on earth did they get any business? Their accounts were certainly up to date, with the most recent filing made only a few months earlier, which made it all the more mystifying. I did, however, have an address, in a leafy road full of semi-detached houses in Wembley. (Of course! Reggae: The Sound of the Suburbs!) Unfortunately, when I tried to use that address in conjunction with either of the names of the directors of the company, nothing showed up on directory enquiries. Now I could have simply gone and knocked on their front door, but that didn't really seem right. So instead I wrote another letter. But I wasn't going to hold my breath waiting for an answer.

Meanwhile, I had another bash at tracking Tex Johnson down. Maybe I could locate some contact details for him via another of his websites? So I did another search for 'Top Rank Media', combined with 'Tex Johnson', and this time I found a site called 'Self Improvement Millionaires', which sounded promising. Well, I could always do with a bit of extra cash in these straitened times, so it had to be worth a look.

I couldn't quite work out what he was selling, but it seemed to be to do with franchising the sales of self-improvement reports – whatever they were. There were certainly some splendid graphics available. I particularly liked the chap in a suit leaping up and clicking his heels together whilst punching the air at the same time ('GOAL REALIZATION MADE EASY'), although I found the picture of 'THE OBESITY TERMINATOR', all baby-oiled six-pack and T shirt ripped to shreds, oddly familiar. I have a friend who writes gay romances and I'm sure I've seen that bloke – or someone very much like him – on one of her covers.

Anyway, I wasn't there to buy, just to scour the site for other information, and indeed the registration details gave me an address and a mobile phone number. Further searches based on this phone number threw up a bizarre selection of other sites that Tex was involved in, such as 'Surveys for Cash', which seemed to be a portal to places where you could indeed undertake marketing surveys for cash. In fact, it seemed at one point as if Tex Johnson was running half of the internet. Obviously I called the number, but it went straight to an automated message that asked if I wanted to leave a text saying I'd called. It seemed easier just to text the number conventionally, so that's what I did. To be honest, I wasn't expecting an answer and I was by this time mentally gearing myself up to going round to the address where the website was registered and doorstepping him. I had come too far to fail now.

I also had one last go at contacting Ciyo Brown. Having failed to get through to him via the message box on his website, I had another sift through the other pages on the site and came across a conventional e-mail address. So I e-mailed that one, explaining that I'd been trying to get in touch via Facebook and all that and that I really, really would like to get on touch, because it would be terrifically good for everyone concerned.

166

And then something COMPLETELY unexpected happened, because half an hour later I got a reply. From Tex Johnson. Sorry, I'll say that again. I GOT A REPLY FROM TEX JOHNSON. I guess I should have expected that, because Ciyo's website is run by Global Music Promotions, and their website is yet another one that's registered to none other than Tex himself. His e-mail simply said that it was nice to hear from me, commenting that it was a shame that so few authors wanted to write about the UK reggae scene. There was a world of talent there and Dennis was one of the most gifted, with a unique voice and style. He would be only too happy to talk to me.

The penultimate domino had just toppled over.

Small, Brown and Grey
and Unobtrusive

So where did this stupid surname come from, then? The popular theory among those of us who are forced to live our lives under it is that it derives from a variant of the word Dunnock. Ornithologists will recognise this as *Prunella modularis*, otherwise known as the Hedge Sparrow and it gets a massively exciting write-up on the website for the Royal Society for the Protection of Birds:

> *A small brown and grey bird. Quiet and unobtrusive, it is often seen on its own, creeping along the edge of a flower bed or near to a bush, moving with a rather nervous, shuffling gait, often flicking its wings as it goes. When two rival males come together they become animated with lots of wing-flicking and loud calling.*

Doesn't that just set the pulse racing? Small, brown and grey and unobtrusive with a nervous, shuffling gait and a predilection for wing-flicking.* However, this still doesn't explain how it came to

---

* As a side note, the bird's apparently modest demeanor led the nineteenth century clergyman Rev Francis Orpen Morris to encourage his flock to 'Be thou like the Dunnock – the male and the female impeccably faithful to each other.' In this, however, he was quite spectacularly wrong. My daughter, who has a degree in Zoology and hence knows about these things, tells me that Dunnocks turn out to have remarkably loose morals and like nothing more than to engage in frantic group sex after a long day's foraging. However, we will draw a discreet veil over this. There may, after all, be children reading.

be adopted as a name – unless, I suppose, it was applied to someone who was particularly small, brown and grey and unobtrusive.

When I was going through my father's old papers, I came across an extraordinary flight of fancy written by my grandfather, Archibald 'Pop' Pinnock, in which he speculated on how the name might have come to be used to describe the occupation of 'pinnock-catcher'. This person would have been given the task of capturing as many as possible of these small birds with the aim of re-sale to pie manufacturers. I liked the old guy even more after reading this, because it was clear from it that he was quite bonkers, and I really wish he could have lived long enough to bounce story ideas around with, even if this would have meant him carrying on until he was in the region of one hundred and twenty years old.

Obviously, I have searched the internet for other suggestions as to the name's origins, but opinion seems divided. There's some interesting stuff on the Internet Surname Database site, where it suggests that it's a locational name from a place called Pinnock in Gloucestershire, just north-east of Cheltenham. This place – which now only exists in the shape of Pinnock Wood Farm – derives from the ancient British word 'pennuc', meaning 'little hill'. Take note of that: 'little hill'. Not mountain, peak or crag, but 'little hill' – essentially the geographic equivalent of 'small, grey and brown and unobtrusive.' There was a pattern emerging here, so I looked elsewhere.

Other sources tend to point towards Cornwall, which is where you find the hamlet of St Pinnock. I have visited this place, and I have to say it was a massive disappointment – the church was barred and bolted, and there didn't seem to be anything much else there at all. On the other hand, I can at least say that, unlike 80s hit chanteuse Charlene, I have actually been to me.

However, the existence of a St Pinnock is potentially quite interesting, even if he does turn out to be one of those saints that no-one seems to know much about. I don't know, but if I was in charge of a religion, I'd make damned sure that I knew who all the saints were, just in case one or two dodgy ones found their way in when I wasn't looking. Then again, given that there are somewhere between 10000 and 20000 recognised saints, there are almost certainly one or two imposters in there.

At this point, I really wanted to reproduce the 33-word entry about St Pinnock that appears on the Catholic Online website ('INFORM – INSPIRE – IGNITE'). So I wrote to them and asked for permission. They sent me a form, which I duly filled in and e-mailed back to them. A couple of weeks later, they gave me their considered verdict, which was that after thorough review, Catholic Online ('INFORM – INSPIRE – IGNITE') were unable to grant me a license at this time. They also took pains to remind me that all material on the Catholic Online website, including presumably that 33-word entry about St Pinnock, is protected by US and International copyright law and cannot be republished without their consent. The missive concluded with the charming sign-off 'Thank you and God Bless, Customer Service.' I think the comma is deliberate.

I had to ask a number of individuals and organisations for permission to use their copyright material for the purpose of this book, but I have to say that Catholic Online ('INFORM – INSPIRE – IGNITE') is the only one who explicitly refused. Still, it hardly matters, as that 33-word entry on their website essentially says that they haven't got much of a clue whether or not St Pinnock existed or even if he was actually someone else altogether. What it amounts to is that St Pinnock is essentially a small, grey and brown and unobtrusive saint.

However, I think we can do better. In my researches, I came across an utterly brilliant saint called Paula the Bearded, who it seems grew a magnificent beard in order to preserve her virtue when pursued by a lustful young Roman, some time in the fourth century. The odd thing about her is that she doesn't appear in any official religious or historical sites at all, which makes me think that she's almost certainly an internet myth, probably based on the equally odd story of St Wilgefortis – who apparently grew such a beard in order to escape marriage to the King of Sicily. This does at least have a bit more of the ring of truth to it. A decent beard takes a while to grow – especially for a woman – and doesn't just sprout spontaneously when you're cornered by a randy centurion.

The thing is, the stories of some saints are so inherently odd that I can't help feeling that it wouldn't be too hard to give St Pinnock a much more interesting backstory and plant it on the internet. What do you reckon? Will you help me with this? Forget the old, dull St Pinnock, here's the new model:

> *St Pinnock of Liskeard (also known as St Pinnock the Flamboyant, St Pinnock the Pungent and St Pinnock the Trouserless) is the patron saint of Milton Keynes, Heligoland and headlice. He is also patron of nuisance callers, PERL developers and the worried well. St Pinnock is noted for the so-called Miracle of the Unwanted Cheese, wherein he succeeded in making an entire village's cheese surplus disappear on a regular basis. He was canonised a few years after his martyrdom at the hands of a group of local dairy farmers following a dramatic fall in sales to neighbouring communities. His feast day is July 15th [Hey, it's my birthday, indulge me – JP]*

Are you with me? Let's do it, then. If you've got a blog, post the above on July 15th and we'll see what happens. St Pinnock deserves this, right? In fact, if we do it properly, I think he'd be a shoo-in as a replacement for patron saint of England, because old

Georgie-boy is, frankly, a bit stretched, what with at least seventeen countries and over twenty cities to look after, to say nothing of boy scouts, syphilitics and people with skin diseases. It's a tough life being a saint.

Dennis Goes Boom Bastic

After Dennis' brief foray into Sugar Minott's territory, he came back to Tex Johnson for three more records. The first of these was a 12" back on Discotex Records, which had acquired a new label design and was now up to catalogue number DT39. For once, Dennis is doing an out-and-out cover of someone else's record – in this case, 'Unbreakable' by Don-E, which was a minor soul hit in 1992. Production is by Tex Johnson and it's arranged by Devon Allison.

It starts off EXTREMELY unpromisingly with a rat-a-tat-tat on a drum machine, making the listener wonder if it was in fact Dennis himself who'd got one for Christmas. Fortunately, this time it's much further back in the mix for most of the record and the song is allowed to come to the fore. It's not a bad performance at all and the plaintive style suits Dennis down to the ground. Having listened to Don-E's much slower original, I'd have to say that Dennis' version is vastly superior, with a much richer timbre to his voice than Don-E's rather weedy delivery.

The B side is a bit of an oddity. It has the truly dreadful title 'Sax Appeal', conjuring up images of dodgy seventies lounge music. Unfortunately, the actual performance, by Winston 'Saxton' Rose, also conjures up images of dodgy seventies lounge music. It is, despite the writing credits, which go to D. Allison / W. Rose, a saxophone solo instrumental version of 'Unbreakable', and it really wouldn't sound out of place on a James Last LP. The only good thing about it is that Dennis isn't tarnished by being associated with it and what's more, he's even taken his drum machine away with him.

For some time I was convinced that Dennis Pinnock's next record was on yet another different label – in fact, I was convinced it was not on a label at all. This is because it has, quite literally, a white label, on which the contents of each side have been stamped using what appears to be a John Bull Printing Outfit. However, as I was trying to sort the records into some kind of order, the presence of the catalogue number 'DT 50' made me think otherwise as this is clearly a tryout for Discotex records – one that clearly never came to fruition because no proper copies of the record ever seem to turn up.

Side A1 is called 'Loyalty' and Side A2 (bets clearly being heavily hedged at this stage) is called 'We Can Make It'. Apart from Dennis' name and the catalogue number, that's all there is to go on. There's no hint as to the producer, composer, arranger or anything. Still, it doesn't matter as long as the content is OK, right?

Well, the bad news is that Dennis has once again brought his drum machine along, and it is as irritating as usual. The only other accompaniment is provided by a trumpet and some spiky keyboard chords. It jogs along at a brisk pace, but it all sounds a bit thin. Now it could simply be that this wasn't anywhere near the final version, but given the way things were going, with Dennis trapped in that special circle of hell reserved for synthetic drummers, I can't help feeling that it was ever going to get much more interesting.

But once again, with the right production it could have been so much better. The tune's great, the horn work excellent and the lyric – presumably by Dennis himself – is actually rather sophisticated:

They want to see you leave me,
They don't understand your loyalty.
They want to see you leave me,
They got a problem, baby, can't you see?

Certain friends of yours,
Keep knocking on the door,
Concerning their selves with our affair.

They say I hold you down,
They claim I play around,
But deep down they know our love is true.

But I'd see them in hell first
Before I lose you,
I'd see them in hell first,
That's how much I love you.

In many ways, this is one of Dennis' strongest songs and it's a damn shame that it's so badly served by the production.

If it were down to me to choose, I'd definitely go for 'Loyalty' as the A side, because 'We Can Make It' … well, doesn't make it. If the production on Side A1 is thin, on Side A2 Dennis gets about as much support as he would from a sheet of wet rice paper. It's desperately weak. The trumpet has gone home, leaving just the drum machine and the keyboards, which plonk along in an uninspiring manner with the occasional odd theremin-like wail in a half-hearted attempt to spice things up. Even the song is pretty poor by Dennis' standards and it's actually quite hard to pick out much of a tune. Not good. Not good at all.

Dennis' final record with Tex Johnson, is, however, rather bonkers. It's called 'Crackula', and it's on the entertainingly-named Boom Bastic Records (12", catalogue number BBR01). As far as I can tell, however, it's the only record on that particular label. Production is by Tex Johnson and Drumie – who may be either Drummie Zeb of Aswad, who is indeed also known for his production work, or Tony 'Drummie' Matthews of Tradition or indeed someone else altogether. There's no date on the record, but given that the telephone number listed on it starts with 081, it would be some time before 1995.

The record starts with an ominous chord, followed by one of those descending scales that indicate that the cartoon baddie is about to make an appearance. Then the beat starts up – a more conventional reggae boom-chukka boom-chukka beat than we're used to hearing on Dennis' records – over which we get a burst of maniacal laughter. OMG! It really IS the cartoon baddie!

Actually, it isn't. It's Dennis. But once it's done we launch into an odd sort of call-and-response, whereby the chorus shouts out 'Crackula!', to which Dennis replies something about vampires. After a couple of these, he starts the main theme, which is all about 'you see nobody don't smoke weed no more' and 'it seem that crack take over now.' So it's a song with a serious message, despite the fact that the lyrics are actually very hard to make out as well as the fact that the backing is regularly punctuated by the sound of a laughing bag being tickled. Thankfully, there is no drum machine, although the backing is a little pedestrian, punctuated by little bursts on what appears to be one of those cheap Casio keyboards.

It's a very odd record indeed, and the B side, 'Para Cat Dub by The Dub Squad' is even odder, because it's basically the same as the A side without Dennis' main vocal and without that it's just a plonking backing track interspersed with odd shouts of 'Crackula.' I would have really loved Dennis to have cut one more ace disc with Tex Johnson – something of the calibre of 'So In Love' perhaps – but unfortunately we'll have to take this curio as their swansong together.

Cornering the World's Vinyl Supply

When I finally sat down to write this book, I thought I already had pretty much everything that Dennis Pinnock had recorded, apart from one particularly obscure number that had only turned up on eBay once, back in 2007 when I'd bailed out at £8.99 only to see it finally sell for £9.49; that one never turned up again on eBay and took some serious detective work on other sites before I finally got my hands on a copy. But I hadn't banked on three more singles turning up in searches during the writing process, along with two Discotex compilation LPs plus that horribly rare Raiders thing that I haven't even mentioned yet, to say nothing of a second Four In A Row single and three different editions of the Eargasm record.

The problem that this presented was that the postman kept delivering them, in full view of the rest of my family. Up until then, I'd managed to spread them apart, even timing the deliveries for when Mrs P was at work, so that full knowledge of my unusual habit was safely kept out of sight.

'Have you embarked on a quest to buy up the world's remaining stock of vinyl?' she said to me one day. I felt this was slightly over-stating the case, but I kept my cool.

'Ha, no. Just filling a few gaps, dear.'

'Hmmm. How much did you spend on this one?'

'£9.99.' I saw no reason to mention postage charges.

'Where do you get them from?'

'Oh, eBay, GEMM, Discogs. You know.'

Then I had an idea.

'When this book is published, they'll be worth, like, LOADS!'
I said. However, I could tell that even this attempt to invoke the
virtues of insider dealing was falling on deaf ears. I needed to try
a different approach.

Later that day, when we were preparing the evening meal
together, I snuck on the latest disc of Dennis' that had just
arrived, 'So In Love'. There was no comment whatsoever as it
played, so at the end I casually remarked:

'Dennis Pinnock, The Soul Years.'

'Oh, so that's him?' she said, looking up from skinning some
salmon. She seemed surprised. And ever so slightly impressed. I
acted all nonchalant.

'Higher voice than I was expecting,' she added. But she was
obviously interested.

The door was clearly opening slightly, so I wedged my boot in
it, quickly fetching the Eargasm 12". The thing is, Mrs P knows
her music. When we first met, she had an excellent collection of
old Motown and Atlantic singles and LPs, and she set me right
about a whole load of misconceptions I'd previously had about
soul. Although I do have to say that lately she's picked up an
unexpected interest in northern European goth metal from our
son. None of us really knows quite how to react to this –
especially said son – but the general consensus is that it's pretty
cool, even if it means that I am having to learn how to
distinguish, say, *Nightwish* from *Within Temptation* in order to avoid
being left by the wayside. I used to think I knew everything there
was to know about music, but it seems there's a whole new world
out there that sprang up when I wasn't looking.

Eargasm went down very well, reminding her of The
Temptations. This was obviously the cue for me to get Four In A
Row's 'Crazy Kind Of Love', because if that sleeve isn't a picture
of a band trying to look like The Temptations, I don't know what
is.

'They're not in a row,' she said when I returned to the kitchen.

'Ah, hold on, I'll get "Love Is…" They're in a row on that one – '

'It's OK, you don't need t– '

But it was too late. I had already gone to get it, along with 'Dennis The Menace'. And maybe a couple of other ones. I couldn't stop myself.

'Um, you're getting a bit intense,' she warned, but her protest was in vain. And, truth to tell, she was – despite herself – actually quite intrigued, and spent the whole of 'Love Is…' trying to work out who his voice reminded her of.

'Now do you see why I'm so fascinated?' I said, finally.

She said nothing. Then again, she may have nodded slightly. Either way, it was enough to be going on with for the time being.

Meeting Mr Discotex

I have to say I'm not a big fan of gated communities. I can see why they exist and I can understand – I think – why someone would want to live in one. But there has to something not quite right about a society in which one group of people feel the need to be protected 24 by 7 from another one. However, having said all that, it is oddly cool to find someone like Tex Johnson living in such a community, if only because the colour of his skin and his origins on the wrong side of the tracks would under normal circumstances put him firmly in the second of those groups. For the same reason, I would also absolve him from the ire I tend to reserve for folk who feel the need to drive expensive cars with personalised number plates. I'd even go so far as to be outraged – although not remotely surprised – at the fact that he tends to get pulled over more often than the statistical norm when driving said car, and wryly amused – not to say impressed – by his response. Which is to politely give the cop in question the contact details of his accountant.

You could say that Tex Johnson is making a bit of a statement by choosing to live where he lives and to drive the car that he drives, but he is – no two ways about it – a self-made man. He grew up in the East End of London, and was – by his own admission – a 'bit of a naughty boy' at school – 'not in fights or anything, but doing things I shouldn't have been doing, in sweet shops, comic books and what have you.' Then, as he says, 'you know when you're always looking … you know when you want to do something but you don't know what you actually want to do? And I just discovered music lessons at school, and that was a way to get out of studying Geography and stuff.'

So he started learning the trumpet and fortunately for him, the teacher realised he'd got a bit of an ear for music. From there it was a short hop to playing sound systems, grabbing the mike at school get-togethers and enjoying the acclaim of his peers, singing along with Linval Thompson and the like. To me, the really interesting aspect of this is that Tex's involvement with the sound systems got him fascinated with how DJs such as Shaka and Coxsone managed to get such a big sound coming out of their speaker stacks. And that led him to the world of valve amplifiers, capacitors and transistors – and in order to understand them, he needed to understand the physics, and in order to understand the physics, he needed to get to grips with the Mathematics. So Tex went back to his school books and got to work on his times tables. I only mention this in passing because it strikes me as an interesting reminder that all learning is connected and that anyone who tries to tell you that there's no point in studying the Arts has no idea what they're talking about. I would imagine you could pretty much draw a direct line between Tex picking up his trumpet for the first time and him becoming a successful entrepreneur.

Having established that he could not only carry a tune but carry it well, Tex's next step was to find some way of getting his work recorded. He took to carrying a cassette recorder around with him, singing new ideas into it at every opportunity, including – and this is a lovely image – when he was on the bus. His approach was a little different to the norm, in that he decided pretty much right from the start to take control of the whole process, setting up Discotex records as his vehicle for doing so. However, crucially for his future relationship with Dennis Pinnock, he didn't immediately assume all the risk; instead, he

went to Tyrone's Venture Records to help put out his first 12"
single. This was called 'I Wanna Hold You All Night Long', and
its catalogue number was EAR 17, putting it right slap bang next
to the 12" version of Dennis' 'Take It Cool' (EAR 16) – although
it was actually released at the same time as Norman Star Collins'
'Let Me Go'. I only mention this because the latter record has the
splendid catalogue number SEX 1, which presumably means it
has not just one but TWO bonking sides.

After hearing what Snoopy had had to say about his relationship
with Tyrone, I was interested to hear Tex's opinion, and – as I'd
pretty much expected – as a producer and label boss himself, he
turned out to have a slightly more nuanced view. I do have to
say, however, that our discussion of Tyrone was still prefixed
with the phrase 'Tyrone's a lovely guy, but…'. Anyway, here's
what Tex said, choosing his words pretty carefully:

'You know, I don't like to be too condemning in any way of
producers in some sense. As an artist I'm unique because I can
see things from an artist perspective, a producer's perspective and
a record label perspective. I wear many hats, and the producer /
the record label – which most producers back then were, the
producer was usually the record label proprietor – tend to get a
lot of stick – sometimes deservedly, but a lot of times, not so.
For example, it's very easy for an artist to assume that their
record has sold lots of copies because they're hearing it played on
Rodigan or Tony Williams, or these days they may hear it on a
pirate station. Back in my days, or the 70s, when records were
selling, however even the biggest of records – the really big all-
time massive records – that were just hits within the reggae
community may have sold only fifteen, twenty thousand. That
was a lot of records for a reggae record back then – that was
enough to hold number one for months.

'When the business got worse, by the late nineties and stuff,
you could sell a couple of thousand records and be at number

one for months. Two to three thousand records and no-one can shift you, and that is a UK hit. Now, because the producer back in those days had to go into the studio with a band of session musicians, pay for studios – which used to be about twenty or thirty pound an hour – master tape, maybe take two or three sessions to get one single together, and then had to find money to manufacture and press, and if you paid artists a little advance, even if that was two or three hundred quid, with two or three thousand record sales, if you see a grand – after expenses – you're lucky.'

I can't say I had the necessary figures to hand to challenge any of this, but there was more than a ring of truth to it. Later on in our conversation, Tex said something that was even more revealing – even if it was, weirdly, in the context of building a career by focusing not on making money but on helping artists: 'If an artist says "My Mum says I should have been paid a million pounds", because they heard their record on the radio, I sit them down and say, "Listen, tell Mum to come around. Sit down, and I'll show your Mum how this works." "Yeah, but Tex, I should have got more than this. What are you going to do?" Mum comes round, Dad comes round, no problem. I say, "You know what? I've pressed five hundred records, in storage I think I've got about two hundred and fifty. This man got fifty, that man got a hundred, here's what I'm going to do. Come to the garage with me. Here's a hundred. That's yours. Take them. Sell them. When you've sold them, keep that. Keep the money. If you need any more, come back and see me." And when you throw it like that, back on them, people start scratching their heads and "All right, all right, Tex. When can we make the next record?"'

This little vignette has so much telling detail in it that I'm sure it must have actually happened at least once and I have to say I have a sneaking admiration for Tex for having the balls to face down not just his artists but their mothers. Those women are *fierce*.

Tex hasn't seen Tyrone since he licensed 'The Feeling' from him for 'Out The Lights, Volume 2' back in the nineties. The only new nugget of information that I managed to glean from Tex was that Tyrone was apparently now living in Luton, just up the road from where I was living at the time, in fact. However, my subsequent attempts to pin him down any further failed completely. There certainly was someone with Tyrone's real name of Barrington Rowe on the Luton electoral roll in 2006 and 2007, but he disappeared off the face of the earth after that.

Tex wasted no time in moving on after just one recording with Venture to take control of the whole of the process himself. Discotex Records was launched into the world soon after, with Tex's own song 'Pillow Talk' taking the DT 1 spot in the catalogue. Not long after that, he began expanding the operation to include work by other artists, including people like Peter Hunnigale and Dennis Pinnock himself. And that's how the awesome Four In A Row came into being, before disintegrating again after only two singles.

Tex refers to FIAR as 'an enjoyable project', and when I remark that it's a shame they didn't make any more records, Tex says that 'everyone was pulling in different directions, and with vocal groups, you've all got to be going in the same direction'. He did want to do an album, but they all had their own projects and they just couldn't keep the unit together. In any case, he was always more interested in the process of making the records and then marketing them than performing – which ties in very well with my earlier observation of his awkward body language on their photo shoots, although I must admit I chickened out of repeating this to him.

I do get the feeling that there's maybe a small part of him that still hankers after getting the band together again one more time, though, despite the fact that he hasn't sung in a studio for over a decade. Ironically, he does now own the studio that he was always desperate for when he was singing – in fact he's owned one for the last ten years – but he's never had the time or the inclination to use it to record his own work. But, as he says, 'the way I look at things, music is good in a sense because when you sing, you can go on for years singing – you don't have to retire when you hit sixty-five – but I want to see some of the kids coming through. Where reggae is concerned – especially in the UK – there's not enough. When I started singing, I made my first record when I was about eighteen or nineteen, but there's not many kids of that age coming into reggae in the UK now. The kids aren't interacting with anything any more, so we've got to keep it alive.'

Tex goes on to say that he reckons that what they created with Lovers Rock is a genre with a unique sound that very few people in Jamaica could capture – in the same way as it's hard for UK artists to create the dancehall style or the real Roots style of Burning Spear, for example, because they haven't grown up in the ghetto. 'Lovers Rock has a very identifiable UK stamp on it,' he says, 'and it never really got its just reward.' I comment that very few songs crossed over, and he agrees but adds that when they did, they stood out a mile. 'Given the chance,' he says, 'it's got just as much substance as good, classic soul, and – if given the chance – it could stand in its own right with the best of them.'

One thing he adds which is interesting is that 'maybe the guys who were responsible for releasing the music at the time' – and that would have included Tex himself – 'just didn't have enough, or put enough in, to try and make it chart when it was easy to do so. Trojan broke people like Ken Boothe and one or two others and occasionally people like Boris Gardiner got through and Sugar Minott and Janet Kay got through, so it just shows you that when the right tune at the right time came along with the right people behind it… All it means is that if you've got a tune back then that was popular on the reggae circuit – number one for two or three months – all it needed was someone who was prepared to put their hand in their pocket. To chart a track you've got to get pluggers on the go and you've got to get street teams and you've got to take it to that other level, you have to print posters on the street and take a few DJs to lunch – know what I mean – to make it happen. And many guys in the business would say why spend £10K when it might not work?'

I put it to Tex that so much of reggae in the UK was like a cottage industry with lots of little labels and he agreed, adding that in one sense, 'that's what's so great about the industry, because if you loved it and believed in yourself, it wasn't any big thing to set up a label and start churning them out. There was enough talent out there – people wanting to record. I was different from most – I wasn't ever a household name in terms of the cream of the crop, but I was one of the first to produce myself as an artist. I released and promoted myself, and there weren't many bands or artists back in the late 70s or early 80s that did that.'

In his time, Tex has run 'fifteen or twenty-five' record labels (I guess you do lose count after a while), covering all genres of dance music, including techno, jungle, drum'n'bass, r'n'b and rap as well as reggae. He seems to have a pretty broad taste in music, and there was a nicely surreal moment in our chat where Tex was enthusing about Queen and The Bee Gees, telling me he would say to his artists 'Listen to that! Listen to the harmonies!' He also turned out to be a big fan of Karen Carpenter, which I really hadn't anticipated at all.

Discotex itself ran from around 1981 to 1992, with its last release in fact being Tex's second album 'That's Life' (which according to a copy of an Echoes chart that I found lurking on a German website was 1993's 23rd highest-selling reggae release in the UK – somewhat higher than I'd imagined). More recently, he's been working as a web entrepreneur, involved in stuff like the sites I found on my internet searches for him. His latest venture, 'Brand New Music Releases', is an interesting proposition that I'm not sure I entirely understand. He seems to be attempting to somehow combine the group-buying features of Groupon, plus a commitment to buying a quota of music per month, on one side of the deal, and training, production and marketing facilities to artists on the other. Much of the training involves things like the Jeff Walker Product Launch Formula, which I would really love to tell you more about except that it's the kind of thing that tends to make me want to chew my own elbows off. Google it if you're interested – you'll probably end up being far richer than me as a result.

I suspect, however, that it suits Tex very well. He is a natural salesman and – I suspect – damn hard-working with it. I guess it could all be smoke and mirrors, but I don't think so. One final anecdote sums up the way he works. 'People used to laugh at me,' he says, 'because I used to walk the streets with Sainsburys and Tesco bags selling my records. But you see the thing about me, it never bothered me people laughing at me, because I wasn't robbing no-one, I wasn't mugging nobody, I was doing something that I enjoyed and you can laugh at me as much as you want, but this race is not for the swift. And the same people I saw laughing at me – if they could see me now...' Tex cracks a big smile and makes an expansive gesture. He knows he doesn't need to finish the sentence.

A Slice of Life

As of early 2012, Dennis Pinnock's last appearance on record seemed to be on the flipside of a single, 'Ain't Got No Love', by Peter Hunnigale. Technically speaking, it's actually Side AA, but given that he's also forced to share it with Sweet Nap's 'Know Your Name', I think we can safely categorise it as a B side. Also, Peter Hunnigale a.k.a. Mr Honey Vibes, is a lot more well-known than Dennis, and has recorded over a dozen albums. Confusingly, Dennis is actually listed as 'D. Pinnock', but I'm pretty certain it's him – unlike the performer on 'Is Your Love Taken' (Arts Records 12", catalogue number 12 Arts T3) who is almost certainly Delroy Pinnock , although I didn't realised that until I'd bought the damn thing.

This single is on Joe G's Records (12", catalogue number JGD 016) and judging from the 0181 telephone number for the distributors that appears on the label, it came out some time after 1995, around 20 years after 'Idi Amin'. Dennis' contribution to the record is called 'Slice of Life' and it's credited to D. Josephs / D. Pinnock. The producer is D. Josephs for Joe G's Productions and it's published by Joe G's Music. Incidentally, at the time of writing you can still buy the MP3 from Joe G's site, which is more than you can say for most of the rest of Dennis' output.

It's an odd little record, this one. Basically, essentially the same backing track, with minor adjustments, is used for three completely different songs by three different artists. The backing track itself, which is a mid-paced, sunny yet slightly wistful little number with occasional interjections from a reedy organ and a brass section, is also played on its own as the filler on the A side. Presumably this is D. Joseph's contribution to the record, as he is listed as co-writer on all three songs. Peter Hunnigale's version is pleasant enough, but as it starts off with some stuff about the birds and the bees and the midsummer breeze and the fishes in the seas, all I can think of is Basil Fotherington-Thomas of St Custard's saying 'Hello clouds, hello sky', so I'm struggling to take his effort seriously.

As far as I can tell, his track on this record is Sweet Nap's one shot at fame, as his unusual moniker turns up nowhere else at all. His lyrics are more of a straightforward love song about needing to know the name of a girl who caught his eye. It's OK, but it's nothing to base a career on — as presumably Sweet Nap subsequently found out.

Dennis, however — just as I would have hoped and expected — delivers something with a bit more depth. His voice is as smooth as it's ever been and the lyrics are altogether more profound. It's a story about struggling to keep life together, beginning with a verse about a sixteen-year-old girl looking in the mirror and crying as she realises her desperate situation:

'This can't be happening
I've only just begun to live.'
She ain't ready to be a mummy,
she is just sixteen

It's a slice of life
in the ghetto.
I'll serve you a slice of life
in the ghetto.

The next verse is about a man working all his life to put his kids through college, only to have his home taken away when he fails to keep up with his mortgage. It's not quite as epic in scope as, say, Stevie Wonder's 'Living For The City', but it's a thought-provoking piece nonetheless. There's so much ambition here that it's really quite tragic that it's where Dennis Pinnock's career seems to have come to a juddering stop. Another slice of life, I guess.

Sharing the Name

Despite Philip Pinnock's evident financial reverses, other branches of the Pinnock family remained plantation owners in Jamaica for some time, as evidenced by memoirs lodged with Jamaican Family Search from Grace Elizabeth Pinnock (Thomas Pinnock's great-granddaughter, born Shafston, Jamaica, 1822) and George Pinnock (her kid brother, born 1824). Grace's memoir describes in vivid detail how the family got caught up in the slave uprising of Christmas 1831, known as the Baptist War. This uprising, which lasted only 10 days, was crushed with such brutality by the planters' militia that the outrage back in England served to hasten the process of emancipation that began in 1833.

It wasn't long after this that the family, now facing ruin, set sail for England, whence both brother and sister, having failed to settle in the home country, sailed away to make a new life in Australia in 1848. The end of George's memoir, written much later in 1899, is quite poetically sad:

> *My career has not been a successful one. I am now 73 years of age without children and having a wife who for some years has been crippled with rheumatism. My business has left me and I am like an old hulk on a sea shore awaiting the last billow that must break me up and scatter my dissected members.*

Wow. Anyway, the point is that there were still plenty of people with my surname admiring the view from the verandahs of their plantation mansions right up until the nineteenth century abolition of slavery. Anecdotal statistics seem to suggest that at least some slaves took their owners' names, so that would make for a fair few black Pinnocks to start the ball rolling.

So I went hunting through the slave registers for the evidence. The first one I found with the name Pinnock was a chap who was simply called 'Old Pinnock'. While it's an entirely accurate moniker – he had apparently reached the remarkable age of 95 at the time of registration, in 1820 – I can't help feeling it was more than a little demeaning. His owner was one Donald Mclean, which didn't yield any more clues as to where he acquired his surname. However, further research threw up a whole host of Pinnocks, including a Philip (ha!) and the first ever Dennis, in the employ of 'James Pinnock Esquire' in 1817 and 1823. This would almost certainly have been a reference to the estate of the late James Pinnock, nephew of Dog-Face Phil, who would have inherited his father Thomas' plantation in St Thomas in the East.

I did wonder if this was the full story, however. According to the BBC Family History website, the option of choosing a surname was generally only open to freed men and women, and the ones in the register were most definitely still part of their respective owners' workforces. That is, apart from Roger Pinnock, one of James Pinnock's slaves, who is listed in 1823 as having run away. One can only hope he at least succeeded in consolidating his escape.

There are a number of possible explanations for this. First of all, they could have been the offspring of an illicit union between James Pinnock and one of his slaves. Despite the inevitable propaganda put out about white women being raped on an hourly basis by lusty slaves, the reverse was all too often the case. However, if this did happen, any resulting issue would have been marked down in the register as 'mulatto' and all but one of the cases that I found were identified as 'negro'. The exception was a woman called Elizabeth Pinnock, but I find it hard to believe that she would have been permitted to adopt the very same name as her owner's wife.

Alternatively, perhaps these were somehow special slaves in that their owners had conferred upon them their surname in order to mark them out as having some kind of higher status. In some cases, their entire name was changed – for example, the Dennis Pinnock mentioned above seems to have been originally called 'York'. This status didn't seem to have stopped them from being traded on, as in the case of Old Pinnock, who ended up with Donald Mclean.

Apart from this, there were also plenty of other potential Pinnocks listed without a surname at all in the registers to add to the list once they were freed in the 1800s. If indeed the combined slave ownership of the various branches of the Pinnock family was maintained at similar levels to what they were in Philip's and Thomas' day, we are talking about 1000 or so people. Now this isn't to say that they'd all take the name Pinnock; a lot would presumably depend on how they felt about their masters and mistresses, and whether they'd prefer to choose one of their earlier owners' names instead. Either way, it was becoming pretty clear why there were apparently so many black Pinnocks of Jamaican origin in the world.

There it was, then. The original James Pinnock and his new wife came over in 1658 to start a new life in the colonies, bought some land and some slaves, made and lost a few fortunes along the way, before buggering off back to England or Australia in the mid 1800s, leaving the poor blacks very little by way of compensation apart from a pretty damn stupid surname. Thanks, guys.

Perhaps understandably, there has been a movement in recent years towards rejecting such slave names, although this has been mainly a US-based thing encouraged by organisations such as the Nation of Islam. Indeed, Louis Farrakhan himself changed his name from Louis Eugene Walcott, presumably because of the associations with the Walcotts who were a major planter family in Barbados. However, it's interesting that any trivial search for the name Walcott on the internet will – in the UK at any rate – primarily return two names: Theo the footballer, who is English of Jamaican descent, and Derek the Nobel prizewinner for literature, who is mixed race and comes from St Lucia (and, ironically, a descendant of that original planter family). I think that's a nice illustration of the way that a name can be reclaimed and purged of unfortunate historical connotations. These things are never quite as straightforward as they seem.

Long Players

For whatever reason, Dennis never did succeed in getting a whole LP devoted to himself – or indeed either of the groups that he was a member of. However, he did manage to find his way onto a number of compilations. The first of these is a live appearance – the only one of Dennis' committed to disc – on a record entitled (deep breath):

BY PUBLIC DEMAND
RAIDERS MUSIC
Presents
THE FINAL EPISODE OF LIVE AT D.S.Y.C. PT. 3
LIVE
AT
D.S.Y.C
via:
NORWOOD HALL 13-5-83 & LECTURER HALL
TOTTENHAM 1-11-83
Featuring
TIPPER IRE, CHAMPION, DENNIS PINNOCK, COLONEL
FLUX, PETER KING & LEVI, DIRTY DESI, GENERAL T,
LESLIE LYRIC, LORNA GEE, SUSTER CANDY, MISS IRE.

Truth to tell, once it's got that lot out of the way, along with a box announcing that the record features *THE HIT TRACK OF PART TWO, THE COMPLAIN NEIGHBOUR by 'TIPPER IRIE'* as well as the words *LIMITED EDITION*, there isn't a lot of space for anything much in the way of pictures on the sleeve. I'm guessing it didn't take a lot of work to put it together.

This record (Raiders Music, catalogue number RM003), as its name suggests, is the third in a series from what claims on the rear of the sleeve to be the *U.K. First Ever LIVE DANCE HALL SESSION (KING TUBBY, JAMDOWN ROCKERS, SAXON, SIR LLOYD, NASTY ROCKERS & GHETTOTONE)*. I recognise several of the names in brackets as sound systems, but I'm slightly mystified as to the claim to be the first ever live UK dancehall session, as dancehall – at least in Jamaica – was a phenomenon that dated back to the 70s.

Still, the important thing for us is that among the list of artists it does feature Dennis Pinnock, which means that for a Pinnock completist it is an essential purchase, even at the inflated prices that it seems to command – I paid £30 plus P&P for mine via Discogs, but I've seen higher prices elsewhere on the internet. I would, however, suggest that unless you really are a Pinnock completist (and I freely accept that I may be the only person on the planet who qualifies for that description) it probably isn't worth buying unless you happen to trip over it at a car boot sale.

Pinnock's track is called '54-64', although this is in fact just another in the long line of misspellings that seem to have dogged Dennis' career, because it's actually a cover of '54-46, That's My Number', originally by Toots and the Maytals. The title of 'Toots' Hibbert's song derives from his prisoner number during a brief spell in the clink for possession, and the original version is as catchy as pretty much everything by him and the Maytals. Unfortunately, I'm not entirely sure that Dennis does it justice here.

He starts off well enough, introducing the song over some organ backing, and the first bit, about not giving his 'sensimilla 'erb' to the policeman, works fine, resulting in some cheering from the audience. However, at this point, the band stop playing and Dennis starts indulging in some banter with the crowd. Then he starts singing again, freestyling somewhat, with the rest of the band gamely trying to keep up with him. The overall effect is, at best, pretty loose, a bit like a semi-operational dub version that struggles along for a couple more minutes before shuffling off, red-faced, into the distance.

The next two LPs that Dennis appears on are compilations brought out by Discotex records. The first one is called 'Out The Lights Vol. 1' and is credited to 'Various Artiste' (catalogue number DTLP4). Dennis' contributions consist of 'In And Out Of Love' and 'Woman Be Fair' as himself, and 'Love Is' and 'Crazy Kind Of Love' as one of *Four In A Row*. The most remarkable thing, however, about this LP is the cover. First of all, there are – inevitably – sleevenotes. Unfortunately, Tex Johnson's sleevenotes are – like his production style – nothing like as mad as Tyrone's. They are, in fact, a fairly restrained – albeit wordy – paean to the power of lurve, and since there isn't much comedy potential contained therein, I shall pass quickly over them.

However, the cover design (concept by Tex Johnson) is something else altogether. For this, we have to thank our old friend Tony Nero, or 'Ants' as he signs himself here. The good news is that he does actually spell Dennis Pinnock correctly for once, although I'm pretty certain that Paulette Hummingbird – or, rather Huminbird – might have something to say about her name losing two key letters. (Incidentally, her contribution here is 'So In Love', with the exact same backing track as used by Dennis on his frankly vastly superior version.) But it's the picture on the front of the sleeve that's bothering me.

Here's why. The cover – essentially a black and white graphic design with blue and red highlights as per an old school *Blue Note* -style jazz sleeve – depicts a Sexy Lady in a short dress reclining on a sofa in the background, clutching a cocktail glass. There is music issuing forth from an old-school hi-fi stack to our right. And in the foreground is The Bloke, about to pull the cord to turn out a table lamp (yes, as in 'Out The Lights'). The problem is that The Bloke is in something of a state of arousal. No, don't panic! We only see his head and upper torso. However, this means that his excitement has to be indicated in other ways, such as his eyes being crossed and his tongue hanging out. And the really, really BIG problem is that you know just who this reminds you of, and unfortunately it's Alfred E. Neuman, cover star of MAD magazine since 1955. By then the spell has been irredeemably broken.

I should say, out of fairness, that the artwork displayed on Tony Nero's Facebook page – where my message to him remains unanswered, but we'll leave that be – is a hell of a lot better than this effort. If I were him, I'd keep Mr Neuman well away from his CV.

The cover of 'Out the Lights, Vol 2', credited this time to 'Various Artistes' (Discotex Records, catalogue number DTLP 10) is a significantly classier affair, albeit with some oddly sinister undertones. The foreground consists of a stock photograph of a couple seated at a table on which are placed two full flutes of champagne. They are clearly out in the open air, enjoying the last few rays of sunset on a summer evening. In the background, looming over them from the top of a hill (although the perspective is a little hard to establish from the way the image has been put together – we're in a pre-Photoshop world here, and scissors and glue are a little less forgiving) is a somewhat gothic looking mansion. This mansion would also appear to be from a stock photograph, albeit one that may well been previously used for a Stephen King paperback cover. The lady is wearing a dress with an extraordinarily large green bow, suggesting that she has perhaps been wrapped up as a gift for some lucky chap. And here he is, leaning in towards her from behind as she turns in his direction, innocently smiling and with her mouth open slightly. Time alone will tell if his intentions are honourable, but me, I'm getting the bodybag ready.

Dennis only provides two tracks on this compilation: 'Reconsider Me' and – rather surprisingly – 'The Feeling' from his days at Venture. Indeed the latter is properly credited as being produced by Tyrone. I have no idea why Johnson chose to use this instead of one of the other tracks from Dennis' Discotex days – maybe he had a particular fondness for it. The sleevenotes certainly offer no clue, mainly because there are no sleevenotes, apart from a comment to the effect that 'Out The Lights, Vol. 2' is also available on cassette and that Volumes 1 and 2 are 'available together on one big CD (20 glorious tracks on one disc)'. Well, I have that CD (catalogue number DTCD 10) and as far as I can tell it's the same size as most other CDs. But maybe that's not quite what he meant.

For the cover design of the Big CD, Tex has sensibly opted to use the cut'n'paste Stephen King collage from Volume 2 rather than Volume 1's dodgy Mad Magazine graphic. He has also, bless him, made a valiant effort to correct the spelling of Paulette Hummingbird's name, to the extent that she is now at least Paulette Humingbird. Still, what's an m between friends? Dennis' name is at least spelt correctly throughout, which is nice because this record, which came out some time in the early 90s, marks his only ever appearance on full-length compact disc.

There is one other long player that Dennis appears on that has so far eluded every attempt of mine to acquire, and in fact I was in two minds about whether or not to mention it at all. Whenever it appears on eBay it already goes for way more than I'm ever going to be prepared to shell out for it, and I'm more than a little wary of doing anything that's going to increase its desirability.

However, I wouldn't be doing my job if I didn't say anything at all about it, so here goes. I should add that I've pieced this information together from the pictures on various eBay listings and thus can be said to lack a certain authority. The LP is called 'Lovers Dub' and it appeared under catalogue number CUT 7 on the Venture label in 1980. The cover features a line drawing of a couple, arm in arm, reclining on some kind of soft furnishing. According to the label, its full name is 'Lovers Dub – the Original Dubtrack', and it's 'RECORDED IN SENSUAL "DUBSURROUND"!!' (oh, Tyrone, you and your double exclamation marks, I have SO missed you). It's produced by 'Tyrone as The Producer for Harlesden Sound Productions in association with The Tricky Trio.'

Rather wonderfully, the credits are given in the manner of a cast list for a movie. Dennis is described as 'DENNIS PINNOCK (vocals, percussion) THE HERO', whereas Snoopy is 'SNOOPY (vocals, solo organ, acoustic piano, percussion) THE FRIEND'. Tyrone himself is 'BARRINGTON ROWE (vocals, percussion) THE GANGSTER'; read into that what you will. Other contributors are, respectively, THE NARRATOR, THE HEROINE, THE MOLL, THE SIDEKICK, THE CARD SHARP, THE VILLAIN, THE PROFESSOR, THE ACTOR, THE GOVERNOR, THE SECURITY GUARD, THE TAXI DRIVER, THE WAITER, THE BANKER, THE SINGER, THE SECRET AGENT, THE FATHER and THE CHORUS GIRLS. I think that ticks most of the boxes, don't you?

The A side of the disc is described as 'Act One', and it's divided up into five scenes. Scene 1 is 'A Chance of Romance' and is credited to Pinnock/Snoopy. There's no other reference to Pinnock on this side. There are two tracks that mention him on the B side (otherwise known as 'Act Two'), Scene 1, 'You Are Heaven To Me' (credited to Pinnock) and Scene 3, 'Secret Love Affair' (credited to Pinnock/Tyrone). All three song titles are new to the Pinnock canon, which might at first suggest that they are yet more tracks from that album that never happened. However, the snippet of music provided with the eBay auction in question is definitely from the B side of 'Saturday Night Feeling,' which leads me to think – in the absence of any further information – that they are simply old songs re-titled to give the impression of something new.

The End of the Quest

There's something quite important that I haven't mentioned yet. While I'd been in the process of arranging to meet Tex Johnson, something extraordinary had happened. I'd had an e-mail from someone else:

> *This is Dennis Pinnock here.*
>
> *Thank you for your letter regarding Pinnock history, I have always wondered about this myself - I will be happy to meet with you to discuss my music career*
>
> *I can be contacted directly on my mobile ...*

So I picked my jaw up off the floor, called his number, and – thirty years after I'd first encountered his music – I finally spoke to Dennis Pinnock. We chatted briefly and arranged to meet up the following weekend, a couple of days after my meeting with Tex.

When I started this project, I never really thought I'd actually find Dennis Pinnock. To be frank, I'd always seen the most likely outcome as the literary equivalent of one of those Nick Broomfield documentaries, featuring me wandering forlornly around the place with a pair of headphones around my neck, clutching a microphone boom. I was pretty convinced that Dennis would turn out to be either (a) dead, (b) in Jamaica or (c) unwilling to speak to me. Or, quite possibly, all three. So to find myself on a train heading into London with an appointment to meet the guy felt more than a little surreal.

He'd arranged to pick me up outside Stockwell station in

South London. He was 'blue T shirt – glasses', and I was 'striped blue top, brown jacket'. Actually, I was 'striped blue top, brown jacket, shuffling backwards and forwards from one side of the station entrance to the other, desperately trying to avoid making eye contact with the dancing nutter in the orange tracksuit', but by the time I'd typed that, he would probably have arrived. Fortunately, we both recognised each other straight away, shook hands and drove round the corner to his house for the interview. He looked just like the picture from his cover photos – a couple of decades or so older, certainly, but still in good shape.

I began by explaining what the project was all about – as if I could really sum it up in a few words without it sounding really weird – but, in common with both Snoopy and Tex Johnson, Dennis still failed to peg me as a complete madman. Maybe this would work out all right after all. Interestingly, Dennis was the first of the three to ask me what the book was going to be called, and I told him that the working title of the book was 'Take It Cool'. He seemed quite flattered by this, so I'm sure he'll be especially pleased that neither the publisher nor myself have managed to come up with anything better in the intervening time. He also seemed flattered – if not spooked – by the fact that I'd collected every single one of his records over the years, remarking that he'd had to do the same himself, thus making him Lovers Rock's answer to J.R.Hartley.* Come to think of it, we probably ended up bidding against each other at some point, which was a really odd thought.

We started off talking about Philip Pinnock and my theory about how the name crossed over and that naturally led on to him

___

* Or indeed Day V Lately, for younger fans of those Yellow Pages commercials.

talking about his family, who came from the Clarendon area of Jamaica. His father, Harry, came over in 1954 at the age of 29 on a ship that took three weeks to sail over from New York – and subsequent research revealed this to have been the MS Sibajak, of the Holland America Line, docking at Southampton on September 22nd. According to historic meteorological data, September that year was relatively sunny (170.9 hours of sunshine), making up for a really crap August (only 148.9 hours), although October wasn't looking promising for an immigrant from the tropics, with only 88.0 hours of sunshine to look forward to. All that and 'no blacks, no dogs, no Irish' too.

Dennis was born in January 1956, six months ahead of me. He grew up in South London, the eldest of three, right in the middle of Brixton's West Indian community, where he says there was always music all around him. As a child of the sixties, he was exposed to the pop music of the time and Tamla Motown, but in addition to that, his mother, Sybil, was a huge fan of Ska – Prince Buster and so on – and used to buy records all the time (I have to say she sounds well cool to me). For a kid of eight or nine in those days, he was unusually interested in the music and whenever anyone asked him what he wanted to do when he grew up, he'd say he wanted to be a pop star.

What really fired his interest was the Rocksteady period, which had its heyday in the late sixties, and he was desperate to start making records at that time, even though he was only eleven or twelve and Musical Youth were still a decade away from recording 'Pass The Dutchie'. But the guy next door to him used to have a band and young Dennis would go there and jam with him, and I'm guessing he must have been pretty good even then if he was tolerated by the grown-ups. However, his parents quite sensibly suggested that he focus on his studies, so he put aside his career plans for the time being.

When he was in his teens, he started hanging around with a local soundsystem called 'Whopper King', named after an infamous character from Jamaica. His job was to be the 'mike man', where he would toast over the records in the style of celebrated contemporary DJs such as U-Roy, Big Youth and Big Joe. Toasting essentially involved making up spontaneous rhymes with a contemporary relevance to fit the backing tracks – in very much the same way as a present-day rapper. This was his first experience of performing in front of large crowds, and it clearly went down well because word soon got around that this kid had something. As well as the toasting, he also started to incorporate singing into his act around this time.

Then in 1976, they were playing at a dance and, as Dennis tells it, 'somebody said to me there's a guy who's jumping up and saying 'Wow wow wow wow!' and they said 'You know who that is? That's Alton Ellis.' And I said 'Alton Ellis? The reggae superstar?' 'Yeah.' 'Ah, OK.' After I'd finished, he came up to me and he said to me, 'I like what you're doing. Do you work with a band?' I said no. He said, 'Have you ever been in a studio?' I said no. He said, 'Would you like to?' Well, yeah!'

So Alton Ellis took Dennis to Chalk Farm studios, and as he said, his singing style at that time was still a bit raw so Alton suggested he did a DJ, so he had to come up with something to DJ about – which is how 'Idi Amin' came into being. As it happens, he didn't really want to do that one, because he wasn't very politically minded at that point – however, Alton helped him with the lyrics and that was his first release in the can. An odd first release, but a first release nonetheless.

However, by the time he got into the studio with Ellis, Dennis had already recorded his first song for Venture in November 1976, which was 'Ride On' – although Tyrone actually sat on that for a year before releasing it. (Yes, I know I've got the first one for Tyrone down as 'Dennis the Menace' on JA-UK. Just humour me – it gets confusing, right?) Dennis spent the rest of the seventies and early eighties working with Venture as we've already seen.

Dennis' memory of the genesis of 'This Is Lovers Rock' is subtly different from Snoopy's, in that he says that he was the one who first started improvising over the backing track. What he did say is that the reason the rhythm track was there in the first place was that another singer was supposed to be coming along to record over it, but she hadn't turned up and that's why there was some slack time in the studio. I suspect it's one of those cases where success has many parents, and to be honest, I can imagine both of them singing along to it, each one trying to outdo the other, so it scarcely matters who was the one who kicked it all off. He does say that the title was his idea, which I don't think Snoopy did – although I think Dennis' subsequent claim to have invented the term 'Lovers Rock' when he came up with the title is perhaps stretching it a bit. The term had certainly been used prior to that – indeed there was a label of that name around in the late seventies – but it is just possible that this was the moment when it got applied to the genre previously known simply as English reggae music. It's also worth bearing in mind that Sugar Minott's 'Lovers Rock' came out straight afterwards, so the Eargasm record may well have started the bandwagon going.

This was also Dennis' first exposure to vocal harmony work, and he says he learnt a lot from Snoopy's skills there. It was a really good time for Dennis, having his first taste of success in his early twenties and as we know, he was supposed to be making an solo album for Tyrone, as well as apparently an Eargasm album. However, as he says 'we did "Lovers Rock", but… I don't think we… received the financial rewards… let me just say that. Snoopy was quite upset about that – quite rightly – and the group just fell apart.' Dennis became disillusioned as well. He did one more record for Tyrone ('The Feeling'), but he was looking to go in a slightly different direction from before, towards more rootsy, socially aware material and Tyrone wasn't happy with that. Now that artistic differences were added to whatever issues they'd had about money, Dennis and Tyrone went their separate ways.

After the experience with Tyrone and Venture, Dennis became disillusioned with the music business and dropped out altogether until one day in 1986 when a friend of his called Victor Lindsey asked him if he was interested in trying something again. My ears pricked up at this point as I realised that he was talking about a record I'd originally put much earlier in his discography. He was talking about Victor and Victor!

Sure enough, Dennis said that Victor Lindsey and Victor Kinghorn had a rhythm – one that had actually been put together by Peter Hunnigale – and they needed someone to voice something over it. Did Dennis have anything? So he said that he did have, a piece called 'Total Disrespect', which they duly recorded and released, even though it was misspelt as 'Totally Disrespect' on the label. Incidentally, I'm guessing that the name Viking for the name of the label came from wordplay around V Kinghorn becoming Viking Horn. As we've seen with Tyrone's eccentric labelling of the sides of his releases, reggae producers have a bit of a penchant for this kind of thing. Presumably that also meant – for what it's worth – that Victor Viking was Victor Kinghorn, and Victor Dee was Victor Lindsey.

Dennis enjoyed being back in the studio and now felt ready to get back into the swing of things, so when he got a call from Tex Johnson not long afterwards, he was eager to work with him. Dennis had previously met Tex in 1979 outside Tyrone's Gangsterville record shop where they both waiting to talk to the elusive producer about their outstanding payments – as Dennis puts it, 'there was always a long line of people waiting for monies.' Tex wanted Dennis to record a song called 'In And Out Of Love', and that's how his association with Discotex Records began, one which lasted on and off until 1993.

Then Tex put together Four In A Row with Dennis, Paul Dawkins and Keith Douglas. They put together a demo at Ciyo's place, freestyling the lyrics and harmonies before taking it Mark Angelo's studio to record. This was another good time for Dennis, and it's obvious he really appreciated working with such a talented bunch of people. They also got a lot of stage work out of it, which he clearly enjoyed. But he echoed what Tex Johnson said about being in a group, that you all have to be like-minded – and although he and Paul Dawkins in particular were really enthusiastic about the project, unfortunately all four of them were pulling in different directions. From that point on, Dennis decided to stick to solo projects in future.

We talked about his later releases, such as 'Slice Of Life', which he was justifiably proud of. Once again, he'd stumbled into that recording session almost by accident, because he'd been at a dance and one of his friends had persuaded him to take over the mike. Someone in the crowd heard him and asked him if he was still singing. Dennis said 'well, I do some songs sometimes', and the guy said he knew Joe G's and offered to link Dennis up with him. So he went round to his studio in Peckham and Joe G asked him if he had any lyrics and Dennis said he had this thing about three different stories in one, from a kind of ghetto perspective. Joe G liked the song and sent him back home to work on it, with a copy of the rhythm track. Unfortunately, Joe G didn't like one line of the song – it sounded too raw to him, although Dennis said it was sung perfectly – so he asked him to re-record it and that was the version that went out. However, Dennis much preferred the original version and he said to me that he'd really like to re-do it some time.

By the time we'd finished talking, I'd gone through almost all of Dennis' singles discography with him. The one I really wanted to know more about was 'Drifting Away', the one that ended up on the back of that Sugar Minott disc. At this point, he exclaimed that I knew more about his records than he did, because he'd almost forgotten about that one altogether. He basically did it –

almost as a favour – because Tex knew the producer. I mentioned the horrific drum machine and it was clear he wasn't keen on the recording either, because the way the vocal was mixed so low. As he said, 'it could have been better.' It could indeed.

The really interesting thing that Dennis told me is that he was actually working again, putting together an album at last. But this time, he was retaining complete control of the process, paying for his own studio time and putting the results out on his own label. His first single release would be called 'Crying Eyes' and was due out some time in 2012. I asked him if he felt disappointed. This is what he said: 'Y'know what? I do feel a bit disappointed, because initially I was supposed to have an album in the Venture era – that was supposed to be my first album – and also during the Discotex era as well, that fell through. It was really no fault of mine, I had all the lyrics, all the songs written and everything, but it just didn't really materialise. However, I'm not discouraged. People come to me all the time and say, 'Look, we're still waiting to hear an album' – so that's going to be my life's work… I will have a couple of albums out, but they will be on my production. I'm happy to do my own productions now because at least that way I've got more control over what I want to do, more creative control.'

I'd love to think Dennis could finally get some recognition for his work. I really enjoyed meeting him, because he's such a lovely guy and really passionate and knowledgeable about his music. I wonder if the problem was that he was simply such a nice, diffident guy that he was too ready to let others take control of his career, for better or for worse. He made one great comment towards the end of our chat, which you could apply to any area of creative endeavour. 'People say to me, 'Do you still sing? Do you still write songs?' and I always say 'Does a fish still swim? Does a bird still fly?' You can't not. It's in you, isn't it?'

The Meaning of it All

Everything happened exactly the way I've described it here. When I started out on this project I really did have absolutely no idea of what I was going to find along the way, but some instinct told me it was going to be an interesting ride. There were so many different stories woven into it, and it's stories that make us human, after all.

I never did quite manage to establish one way or the other if my bunch of Pinnocks had anything to do with Dog-Face Phil's clan. In some ways, I feel reasonably happy that we've got nothing to do with them, because my folk were of significantly more humble stock than that other snooty bunch. However, some aspects of the geography were worrying and the further back I went, the closer physically the two sets of ancestors seemed to get. One day, perhaps, I'll sort it out once and for all, but the trouble with genealogy is that it very soon becomes an all-consuming obsession and it's not long before you've unwittingly become half of a bickering couple in Stevenage that no-one else seems to want to talk to any more.

I am fairly certain, however, that I've established beyond reasonable doubt how the name became so prevalent among people of Jamaican origin. It's not a pretty story, but I'd like to think there are enough black Pinnocks who have made their way in the world to have purged the name of any adverse connotations. In any case, the history of the white Pinnocks in Jamaica doesn't exactly seem to suggest a happy ever after ending for most of them either. For all his one-time wealth, Philip Pinnock must have had a pretty miserable last couple of years engaged in a lonely fight against his encircling creditors.

As for Dennis Pinnock, after studying his records in depth, I really have come to the conclusion that he may well be the greatest reggae singer that hardly anyone's ever heard of. Certainly a few of his records are pretty terrible – mainly owing to poor choices of material and variable production quality – but most of them are excellent and, frankly, a whole load better than many other efforts that have made a much more lasting impact on public consciousness. He's also exceptionally versatile, able to navigate his way across several different styles of singing with ease, and a gifted interpreter of both his own songs and those of others. He also seems to be held in high regard by his peers – at least the ones I spoke to. But maybe the problem is simply that he was a medium-sized fish in a very small pond indeed. The very area he was working in – Lovers Rock – is a scandalously uncelebrated niche of music, and hardly any of its performers ever broke out into the mainstream. One day, perhaps, this homegrown genre will receive its just reward – it is, after all, about as English as Morris dancing.

Listening to Dennis' records, I can't help feeling that – setting aside any other considerations – the most exciting producer he worked with was Tyrone, because he seemed to have the right level of insanity and innovation needed to bring out the best in him. It is a real shame they couldn't have worked out some way to stick together and come up with that 'Dennis The Menace' album, because that might have changed everything for him. If you have a moment, by the way, do check out a record by Tradition called – in an inspired flight of fancy by none other than Snoopy – 'Captain Ganja and the Space Patrol'. You'll need to find it on YouTube because vinyl copies tend to change hands for hundred of pounds, but it's as bonkers as anything by Lee 'Scratch' Perry and it's probably Tyrone's masterpiece. I'm still quite disappointed that I didn't manage to track him down. For all his apparent faults, he seems such a fascinating, enigmatic character.

I said there were several different stories woven into this project, but I did wonder if there was perhaps a single overarching narrative. About two-thirds of the way through the process of writing, it struck me that it was really a tale about two very different people who shared the same surname: Philip and Dennis Pinnock. Philip was the grandson of a man who had crossed the Atlantic westwards in search of a better life and Dennis was the son of a man who had done exactly the same, but in the opposite direction, two centuries later. However, whereas Philip became implicated in a ghastly trade that blighted the lives of millions, Dennis is an entertainer who has brought joy into a considerable number of peoples' lives over the years. Philip's life was superficially one of glittering success and yet died in miserable circumstances; Dennis's musical career is, by any conventional yardstick, somewhat less than stellar, yet he seems at ease with himself today and he certainly hasn't abandoned his dreams.

I'm probably being simplistic here. But there's a place in history for the little men as well as the big ones, and sometimes those little men can do a hell of a lot more good for the world. Wherever his career goes from here, Dennis has already brought some damn fine records into being and I'm proud to share my bloody stupid but now ever so slightly cooler surname with him.

What Happened Next

The big difference between writing fiction and non-fiction is that with fiction there's always an ending. Even when some idiot like me decides to write an entire unwarranted sequel to your masterpiece (you *have* forgiven me, haven't you, Jane Austen?), your original novel remains a complete, self-contained entity.

Real life is very different from this. Stuff continues to happen, and if you're not careful, you end up in a state of constant re-vision right up to the point when the book goes to press. This book was no exception. I finished it towards the end of May 2012, but it took a further eighteen months of hustling and hassling before it eventually found a publisher. A lot can happen in a year and a half.

The most significant thing is that Dennis made good on his intention to get back to recording, and in August 2012 he sent me a CD of 'Crying Eyes' b/w 'My Baby' on his own Reggaesonic label (which has a rather spiffy logo, featuring the word 'Reggaesonic' in the shape of the profile of a jet fighter). 'Crying Eyes' comes in a very smart cardboard sleeve with a classy photo of Dennis on the front. There are three tracks: 'Crying Eyes', 'My Baby' and 'My Baby (PA Mix)'. It's produced, written and arranged by Dennis, so I guess this makes it his production debut.

'Crying Eyes' starts off with an alarming electronic drum flourish, but fortunately this settles down fairly quickly to its correct position in the mix (as far back as possible), allowing Dennis' jaunty vocals and (I'm fairly certain) Ciyo's guitar to take centre stage. It's a nice, up-tempo tune with a wistful tinge to it, distinguished by some excellent multi-tracked vocals from Dennis, proving that he has most definitely Still Got It. 'My Baby' is a slower number and if anything slightly stronger than 'Crying Eyes', with some lovely synthesized horn glissandi in the accompaniment. There's a gorgeous, warm production feel to it, too, and it's probably my favourite Dennis Pinnock track at the moment. The PA Mix, by the way, is the same thing minus the main vocals.

Later in 2012 he was one of a number of Lovers Rock artists who turned up on an MP3-only album entitled 'Nu-Lovers Uk, Damsels & Crooners Vol. 1'. His contribution is Track 14, 'A Search for Love', and there's no other information about it on either Amazon or iTunes. However, a quick internet search led to a dormant Twitter feed under the handle of Demondok, and this in turn took me to the Myspace of one Derek Fevrier, who turns out to be a reasonably prolific technician and producer both in the UK and the Caribbean. 'Nu-Lovers Uk, Damsels & Crooners' seems to be his baby.

I can't vouch for the other tracks because I was a cheapskate and just bought the one with Dennis on it, but 'A Search for Love' is – to me at least – a backward step. The intro sounds like something Ronnie Hazelhurst might have thrown together on his day off for some long-forgotten 70s sitcom and the rest of it continues in a similar vein. Dennis is a true pro, however, and his vocal is exemplary, even if it does suggest an unexpected potential alternative career working the cruise ships. I'm so glad he didn't come out of retirement just for this, because 'Crying Eyes' and 'My Baby' are so much better.

In late 2013, one more track emerged, called 'Cloud Nine'. Once again, this seems to be part of another MP3-only album, entitled 'Strictly for Lovers, Vol 1', on the DigiTec label. Production is by Gary Lewis, who is basically Mr DigiTec. For once, the music hasn't been specially written for the track; instead, Dennis and his producer have used a 'riddim' (in other words, instrumental) track by Horace Andy (who, incidentally, is not only one of Dennis' vocal heroes, but also a frequent collaborator with Massive Attack). The song itself is fairly pleasant, and it does at least have a proper reggae beat to it, but it doesn't quite set the world on fire. In some ways I'd feel a little sad if this was to be Dennis' swansong and I'd certainly like to think he has a few more tunes left in him. The good thing is that on the back of these new recordings, Dennis has got himself on the bill at several 'Giants of Lovers Rock' gigs, including a couple at London's O_2 arena, so perhaps he may yet get to make that album.

I first started writing this book in 2005, so even if the nature of such projects is that 99% of the time is indeed taken up in prevarication and procrastination, it still feels like I've spent the best part of a decade living with 'Take It Cool'. After all this time, I am quite unbelievably pleased and excited to see it finally make it into print, and I hope that you have enjoyed the journey as much as I have.

Did I really say 'journey'? Oh dear. I think I did.

Discography

Reggae music is notoriously badly documented. Partly this is because it has always been such a cottage industry, with odd little labels continually popping up and disappearing almost as soon as they've established themselves. In that respect, it's always been much closer to the spirit of punk than punk ever was. But mainly it's because no-one's really bothered, apart from the online resources Tapir and Discogs, and even they turned out to be significantly incomplete when it came to Dennis Pinnock. When I met Snoopy, he did say he was in the throes of putting together a proper, definitive discography of reggae – and if anyone can do it, he's probably the man. But I do fear for his sanity.

In the absence of anything better, however, here is my attempt at a discography for Dennis using information gleaned from various websites, the records and Dennis himself. I reckon it's about as good as you're likely to get, frankly.

Solo Singles

1977	Version (B side of Loving You, by Janet Kay)	All Tone 12"	AT 006
1977	Idi Amin / Idi Dub	Conflict 7"	CON
1978	Dennis The Menace / Automatic Crystal Rankers	JA-UK 12"	PFU
1978	Ride On / Rock On	Venture 12"	VNLP 92
1979	Take It Cool / Pinnock's Paranormal Payback	Venture 7"	OWN 1
1979	Take It Cool / Dennis the Menace	Venture 12"	EAR 16
1979	I've Only Just Begun / I Can't Afford To Quit	Venture 12"	EAR 25
1980	The Feeling / Saturday Night Feeling	Ambassador 12"	EMB 7778
1985	Totally Disrespect / Totally No Respect	Viking 7"	VIK 002
1985	In And Out Of Love / In And Out Of Dub (by Disco Tex Band)	Discotex 12"	DT 18
1988	Reconsider Me / Let's Reconcile	Discotex 12"	DT 22
1988	Woman Be Fair / Fair's Fair	Discotex 12"	DT 24

1988	The Feeling / Keeping A Watch Over You (by Elements)	Music Scene 12"	MKS 62549
1988	Drifting Away / Drifter (by Sugar Minott)	Up Tempo 12"	TEMP 028
1989	So In Love / Steel Pan Rock-steady (by Disco Tex Band)	Discotex 12"	DT 28
1992	Crackula / Para Cat Dub	Boom Bastic 12"	BBR 01
1993	Unbreakable / Sax Appeal (by Winston 'Saxton' Rose)	Discotex 12"	DT 39
1994	Loyalty / We Can Make It	White label 12"	DT 50
1996	Slice of Life (B side of Ain't Got No Love, by Peter Hunnigale)	Joe G's 12"	JGD 016
2012	Crying Eyes / My Baby	Reggaesonic CD	RSCD 001
2012	A Search for Love	Nu-Lovers UK MP3	
2013	Cloud Nine	Digitec MP3	

Group Singles

1979	Dennis and Lauraine	You and Me Baby / You and	Soferno B 12"	SOF 007B
1980	Eargasm / P Pop And The Beagle	This Is Lovers Rock / Name That Tune	Venture 12"	EAR 26
1980	Eargasm / P Pop And The Beagle	This Is Lovers Rock / Name That Tune	Venture 7"	EAR 726
1987	Four In A Row	Love Is... / The Essence Of Love	Discotex 12"	DT 19
1987	Four In A Row	Crazy Kind Of Love / A World	Discotex 12"	DT 20
1988	Eargasm / P Pop And The Beagle	This Is Lovers Rock / Name That Tune	Music Scene 12"	EAR 26

Album Tracks

1983	The Final Episode of Live at	54 – 46	Raiders LP	RM 003
	Out The Lights, Volume 1	Love Is (with Four In A Row)	Discotex LP	DTLP 4
		In And Out Of		
		Crazy Kind Of Love (with Four		
		Woman Be Fair		
	Out The Lights, Volume 2	Reconsider Me	Discotex LP	DTLP 10
		The Feeling		
	Out The Lights, Volumes 1 and	Love Is (with Four In A Row)	Discotex CD	DTCD 10
		In And Out Of		
		Crazy Kind Of Love (with Four		
		Woman Be Fair		
		Reconsider Me		
		The Feeling		

Resources

Like any lazy desk-bound person in the 21st century, my principal research tool in writing this book was *Google*. However, it should be noted that there are a number of more sophisticated and specialised sites available.

The mother of all genealogy sites is of course *Ancestry* (www.ancestry.co.uk or your local equivalent), which is pricey but pretty comprehensive and – provided you have some idea of the dates of the person you're looking for – reasonably straightforward to search. It also helps if you happen to have a relatively unusual name like Pinnock. The *Church of Jesus Christ of Latter-Day Saints' Family Search* site (familysearch.org) is also worth a visit, as not only is it free but it also somehow manages to find some stuff that Ancestry doesn't (the opposite of this is, sadly, also true). More specialised still is the excellent *Jamaican Family Search* (jamaicanfamilysearch.com), which is as far as I can tell a one-woman operation curated by the formidable Ms Patricia Jackson. This is a terrific site, full of wonderful anecdotal information and oddball memoirs. Finally, the *FreeBMD* project (www.freebmd.org.uk) is excellent for finding information on births, marriages and deaths registered in England and Wales, and the *Internet Surname Database* (www.surnamedb.com) has some fascinating information on the origins of names.

For music, *Discogs* (www.discogs.com) is becoming the place to go to if you want to find out details of obscure artists' discographies, as well as becoming a marketplace to rival eBay. For reggae in particular, *Tapir's Reggae Discographies* (tapirs.home.xs4all.nl) is also useful, although most of the information is increasingly available on *Discogs*. If you want to find Dennis' records, however, eBay is still probably your best bet, although it's worth checking *Supertone Records*' (supertonerecords.co.uk) catalogue as well (and say hello to Wallie while you're there). *DanceCrasher* (www.dancecrasher.co.uk) also has an excellent archive of old reggae charts (although, frankly, you can't beat having a neighbour (see below) who has a stash of old *Black Music* magazines). The *British Record Shop Archive* (www.britishrecordshoparchive.org) is a splendid, if poignant, resource for finding out information about the UK's vanishing record shops.

I also found the website for the exciting new *Richmond, St Ann* housing development (www.richmondjamaica.com) useful for information on Philip Pinnock's former estate. The *PortCities Bristol* website (discoveringbristol.org.uk) has some excellent material relating to the transatlantic slave trade, including that letter that sent my investigations towards Jamaica. The archive for the *Daily Gleaner* (gleaner.newspaperarchive.com) is a veritable treasure trove of fascinating historical articles, even if it's a bit on the pricey side. Finally, the UK Met Office (www.metoffice.gov.uk) has some excellent historical weather data, and generally speaking it's slightly more reliable than their forecasts.

I also read a few books. James Walvin's *A Short History of Slavery* (Penguin, 2007) is a very readable introduction to the subject. Edward Long's *The History of Jamaica, Or, General Survey of the Antient and Modern State of That Island* (Lowndes, 1774) is interesting to dip into if you can bear getting into the mind of someone who was, as Walvin puts it, 'no friend to the slaves'. The Rev George Wilson Bridges' *The Annals of Jamaica* (John Murray, 1828) is quite a rollicking read for a historical tract and is at times most entertaining. Frank Cundall's *Biographical Annals of*

Jamaica (Institute of Jamaica, 1904) provides some useful thumbnail character sketches along with an equally brief summary of the island's history.

Captain J.H.Lawrence-Archer's *Monumental Inscriptions of the British West Indies* (Chatto and Windus, 1875) is a pathologically obsessive list of epitaphs, along with additional biographical notes where the author feels they are merited, because of either the subject's status or the unusual circumstances surrounding their demise (for example Mary Ann King – died 29th August, 1856 – who was 'poisoned through the mistake of a druggist.') 'The Magazine of Magazines' for July 1754 (Andrew Welsh, 1754) is an insane attempt to produce a digest of EVERYTHING WRITTEN ANYWHERE ON ANY SUBJECT WHATSOEVER for that particular month (and I assume there are many others) and as such is one of the most randomly fascinating documents I have ever encountered. Frank Wesley Pitman's *The Development of the British West Indies 1700 – 1763* (OUP, 1917) has some interesting stuff on the planters of Jamaica, including Philip Pinnock himself. Finally, closer to home, Mary Southall's *A Description of Malvern* (Longman, Hurst and Co., 1822) was useful for information on the Pinnocks before they set sail for the West Indies.

I would dearly love to recommend some good books on the subject of Lovers Rock, but the only one I've come across that goes further than a dismissive mention is Lloyd Bradley's *Sounds Like London: 100 Years of Black Music in the Capital* (Serpent's Tail, 2013) and that had the temerity to be published long after I'd finished writing mine. Bradley devotes the whole of Chapter Six to Lovers Rock in fact, and it's an interesting and informative read, even if he completely fails to mention our man Dennis. Still, an entire chapter is a lot more than the *Rough Guide to Reggae*, which has almost nothing whatsoever to say on the subject. Indeed, if you search for books on 'Lovers Rock' on Amazon, the first result to come up is *Ukelele for Dummies*, which isn't any help at all apart from conjuring up ideas for some truly horrendous cover versions.

Having said that, Menelik Shabazz's documentary film, 'The Story of Lovers Rock' is well worth watching, even if it doesn't feature Dennis, and is far better than any book as a place to start learning about Lovers Rock. Apart from this one, of course.

Acknowledgements

Thanks first of all to my wife, Gail, who didn't sign up to this living-with-a-writer thing when she married me all those years ago, but still puts up with it with bemused tolerance. Thanks to the brilliant Dennis Pinnock, without whom this book would literally have no reason to exist, and also for giving up his time to talk to me. Thanks also to his one-time collaborators Snoopy and Tex Johnson for agreeing to be interviewed.

Thanks, as always, to the Verulam Writers Circle – how I miss you guys! – and all those in it who supported me during this book's long and difficult gestation, especially Ian Cundell, who has been midwife to more books than is possibly healthy for a middle-aged man, and Mary Woodward, who was present when I first read an extract back in 2005 and suggested that the slavery connection might be worth following up. Thanks also to Rob Johnson for tracking down those articles in *Black Music* magazine and for filling in some other important gaps, as well as ensuring that I'm not the only reggae obsessive in the village.* Thanks also to Janne Salonen for the information on *Lovers Dub*, going some way to make up for snatching it from under my nose on eBay.

Thanks to everyone who followed the serialisation of the book on Twitter and Facebook and encouraged me by commenting, re-tweeting or simply liking a post – you have no idea how much that meant. Special thanks to Matt Pinnock

---

* Seriously, who would ever imagine that a tiny village in Somerset would have Rob and myself living across the road from each other? In this part of the world, the Wurzels are the cutting edge of rock'n'roll.

(@MSPinnock), who as far as I know is no relation at all, but who still re-tweeted every single episode. And extra special thanks to the wonderful Ian Rankin for allowing me to use his tweet of encouragement for the cover of this book.

Finally, thanks to the innumerable agents and publishers who reassured me that 'someone will love it' even if it 'wasn't for them', and of course to the lovely Samantha Hawkins of the utterly brilliant Two Ravens Press, who turned out to be that someone.

Dennis Pinnock's lyrics appear by kind permission of Dennis Pinnock.

Extracts from 'Philip Pinnock, the Dandy' and 'Descendants of Pinnock and Grant and Will of Mrs Isabella Campbell' (in 'Dog-Face Phil') and 'Memoir of George Pinnock' (in 'Sharing the Name') appear by kind permission of Jamaican Family Search.

The description of the Dunnock in 'Small, Brown and Grey and Unobtrusive' appears by kind permission of the Royal Society for the Protection of Birds.

The image of the letter from Samuel Munckley to Philip and James Pinnock in 'The Wrong Corner of the Triangle' appears by kind permission of Bristol Record Office.